Il vero italiano:
Your Guide To Speaking "Real" Italian

by
Keith A. Preble & Francesco Rossi

Table of Contents
Indice

Preface
Prefazione

I came up with the idea for Parola del Giorno (http://www.paroladelgiorno.com) at the end of 2006. I had just returned from a trip to Italy, and I was looking for a way to continue learning and improving my Italian. As I became more proficient, I noticed the number of resources for intermediate and advanced students seemed to decline.

I began to find that learning from books and studying lists of words was becoming mundane. These kind of tasks are useful in the beginning when you need a foundation of useful vocabulary to communicate. I soon found that I just could not remember the dozens of words I studied every week, especially on my own.

While brainstorming one afternoon, I remembered two teachers from school: Mr. Toro, who taught Study Skills in the 5th grade, and Mrs. Bannon, my Honors English teacher in the 9th grade. In both classes, we studied how to improve our vocabulary using *context clues*. Every week in Mrs. Bannon's class, we would have to take the vocabulary lists we were using to study for the SAT's and write sentences. Our sentences could not be random: they had to demonstrate that we understood the meaning of the word and, most of all, the meaning of the word could also be deciphered from the context.

I thought to myself: *Can this same technique work in Italian?* I decided to give it a try. I started to keep an Excel spreadsheet of words I was encountering through reading online newspapers and magazines. I would note how the word was used or if there were any special rules or usage. For example, was the noun followed by a preposition? Was it used only with certain verbs? I would then study my spreadsheet during breaks at work.

After a few months, the spreadsheet was becoming cumbersome. I would email it to myself each day so that I would have the most updated copy with me to study at work. After a while, this became problematic. I would often forget to email it to myself or, if I made changes or updated it at work, I would forget to email it back to myself. I soon found myself with dozens of different versions of the spreadsheet.

I realized I needed a better way to manage all of this information. A friend of mine suggested starting a blog and putting all of my research online. I wouldn't need to worry about carrying around a spreadsheet with me and could share my work with other people who might be interested. More importantly, the blog could be accessed anywhere as long as I had an internet connection.

At the end of 2006 just after Thanksgiving, I decided to create my first blog. It did not take long for the site to catch on, and today there are thousands of people who follow our daily updates on paroladelgiorno.com via Facebook, Twitter, our iOS app, Kindle, and via our email digest that goes out each weekday. The site not only has pushed me to continue learning Italian, but it has also encouraged and motivated thousands of others, too!

I hope that this ebook will continue the work I began in 2006 and that you, too can connect with Italian the way that I have.

Dedication
Dedica

I want to thank my very first Italian teacher, Grazia, for all the help that she (and her family) have given me. Grazia helped me to overcome my fear and shyness with the language, specifically with speaking. She pushed me to make mistakes and to have confidence in myself. Without her patience and amazing methods as a teacher, I wouldn't be as *bravo* as I am today (this book certainly would never have been written).

I would also like to thank my friend, Fabio, from Rome. Fabio is the first Italian I ever met, and we have known each other for so many years. Fabio is one of the most patient tutors and friends that I have ever known, and he is always ready to help me improve and learn new things! It is because of him that I have come to know and love Rome so well.

I also need to thank my friend, Danilo, who never hesitates to point out my mistakes when speaking and writing Italian (I lost track of the zeroes!). Our almost daily chats and conversations on the iPhone, Facebook, Skype and even MSN over the years have helped me immensely. I don't think my Italian would have improved as much as it did without his patience and encouragement!

I also want to thank my friend, Francesco, who collaborated with me on this ebook. Francesco has been a tremendous help in growing PdG. Our many conversations have provided useful "fodder" for the blog's daily updates.

Keith Preble
info@paroladelgiorno.com

Authors
Autori

Keith Preble is currently finishing his Masters in Government & Politics with a major in international relations from St. John's University, Rome Campus in Italy. His master's thesis studied the role of multilateralism as an instrument of Italian foreign policy during the Suez Crisis (1955-56). He began his undergraduate work at Clark University (Worcester, MA) and received his Bachelor of Arts from the University of Melbourne (2003).

Francesco Rossi is a native Italian from the city of Palermo (Sicily). He is currently pursuing his Bachelor's degree in music composition at the *Conservatorio Vincenzo Bellini* in Palermo, Sicily. He received his music diploma in piano performance in 2011.

Rome: Roman Forum (2014)

Special Thanks

Lastly, I would like to thank all of the individuals and groups who donated to PdG during its fundraising in May-July 2014. In less than one month, PdG raised more than $2500.00!

This book is a thank you to all of you who made the bold statement: "We want PdG to stick around for a long time!"

These funds are being used to develop and publish an Android app (due out in late 2014) to complement our popular iOS app. The funds were also used to pay our hosting fees, domain fees, and other yearly expenses that we have incurred over the last few years. Maintaining a web site can be costly, and, as the site grows, our demands have grown, too.

This book is not only dedicated to the generosity and kindness of everyone who donated but also to the thousands of people who have visited the site each week and strive to learn and improve their Italian! I am deeply appreciative of the following the web site has attracted, and I hope that it will continue to grow.

Italian is such a beautiful language, and Italy is just as beautiful with its rich history and enduring culture. It is a land that is fraught with problems and hardships, but Italians never cease to amaze me with their patience, generosity, and ability to make the best of any situation.

I hope that through PdG you will come to know *the real Italy (and Italian)* as I have! *Grazie mille!*

How to use this book

This guide is divided into several chapters, each relating to a particular part of speech (**una parte del discorso**). The introduction to each chapter will include some brief explanations of Italian grammar related to that part of speech. Some chapters are more complex than others, especially those on prepositions and pronouns, while others are more straightforward, such as those on interjections and nouns.

After the grammatical introduction on each part of speech, important words and phrases will be introduced relating to that part of speech. Some words and expressions are common to many textbooks on the market while others less so. You are bound to encounter some grammar that is rarely seen in standard textbooks. Words were primarily chosen based on my experiences with them in Italy. Where it functioned in the text, I included anecdotes or experiences related to these words.

We felt that organizing the book in this way made it easier to use as a reference and present the words in a coherent fashion.

We hope that the book presents Italian as it is used every day!

The Italian that we often learn in textbooks and in classes is not the *real language* that one might encounter "on the streets" here in Italy. Like English, not everyone speaks *properly*. At times, what is "proper" Italian to one person is not necessary proper for another. Regional differences and educational disparities between speakers abound in Italy (just as they do in any country). Furthermore, the examples used in this book do their best to show *how* Italian is used in everyday situations.

Many of the words and phrases selected, when used properly, will make you seem less like one of those "textbook" speakers. If used properly, these words and expressions will impress and possibly surprise native speakers, many of whom will not be expecting you to know these words and phrases.

The book is also a compendium of some of the most popular and useful "words of the day" published on my blog, paroladelgiorno.com, since 2006. Care was taken to include a lot of new material, too. Rome has been my home since 2012, and my **vita romana (e italiana)** has given me a unique opportunity to connect with the language in ways that I could never do learning Italian in the United States. Even while studying with a native speaker in Durham, NC (where I must say my Italian really took off), it is no substitute for total immersion. One of the aims of this book was to capture some of what I learned through my language immersion (on average, I only speak English 1-2 hours a day at best and speak Italian the remainder of the time).

I also tried to include as many anecdotal and personal experiences as possible through conversations with friends and acquaintances and through my observations. When introducing examples, I try to create a situation or context where the word or phrase might apply. These situations can make knowing when and how to use words extremely useful as well as aid in remembering them.

What this book is *not*

It should be stated what this book *is not*: this book *is not* a complete and thorough grammar guide. You won't find explanations on how to use every verb tense, and some topics were excluded because they are already well-covered or easy enough, in my opinion, to understand from books and texts already on the market.

Many chapters include **Avvisi** and other grammar notes and tidbits. In the middle of some chapters and at the end of others, you will find sections called **Da notare,** which present important points of grammar that we felt could not be ignored.

This book is best suited for students who already know some Italian. Beginners may find the book overwhelming or difficult to follow. For those who are less interested in grammar, skipping these sections and learning new words can also work.

In bocca al lupo! (*Good luck!*)

Catania: Fontana dell'Elefante in Piazza Duomo (2014)

1 Verbs
Verbi

Verbs in both English and Italian are one of the most vital components in the construction of phrases. Whereas English tenses have two forms of the verb for each tense (*sing/sings, run/runs, jump/jumps*), Italian has six! For many students of Italian, whose first language is English, this can present problems. It can be a lot of work memorizing all of the forms, but most verbs follow predictable patterns of conjugation.

This chapter begins with a brief introduction about Italian verbs and then will look at some important verbs in five categories:

1. Verbs every student *must* know

2. Verbs for daily activities

3. Irregular verbs

4. Modal verbs

5. Pronominal verbs

Forms
Forme

Italian grammar classifies verbs as having three forms:

1. active: <u>the subject</u> performs the action (*The tractor trailer struck the car*).

2. passive: <u>the subject</u> of our active phrase becomes the **patient** of the verb (*The car was struck <u>by the tractor trailer</u>*), resulting in a change of state.

3. reflexive: <u>agent and patient</u> (subject and object) are one in the same (*The baby fed himself*).

Conjugations
Coniugazioni

Italian has three types of conjugations: the first (**-are**), second (**-ere**), and third (**-ire**). Verbs with **-ire** suffixes may also have an infixed conjugation and are often referred to as "**-isc- verbs**" (such as **finire** and **preferire**).

Verbs that end in **-arre, irre,** and **-urre** belong to the second conjugation (**-ere**).

As a general rule, the stress on the infinitive is placed on the suffix of the verb: **amare**, **cadere**, and **preferire**. However, some **-ere** verbs place the stress within the stem, such as **credere**, **prendere**, or **difendere**.

For conjugated verbs, the stress *always* falls on the next to last syllable except for the third person plural: the stress falls in the same place as the third-person singular: canta & cantano, lava & lavano, lavora & lavorano, etc. *This pattern applies to all tenses in Italian.*

The charts that follow illustrate the endings (**le desinenze**) used for each conjugation type in the present tense. These four verbs below reflect *regular verb* conjugation patterns.

cantare: _to sing_

io	cant**o**	noi	cant**iamo**
tu	cant**i**	voi	cant**ate**
lui/lei/Lei	cant**a**	loro	c<u>a</u>nt**ano**

credere: _to believe_

io	cred**o**	noi	cred**iamo**
tu	cred**i**	voi	cred**ete**
lui/lei/Lei	cred**e**	loro	cr<u>e</u>d**ono**

dormire: _to sleep_

io	dorm**o**	noi	dorm**iamo**
tu	dorm**i**	voi	dorm**ite**
lui/lei/Lei	dorm**e**	loro	d<u>o</u>rm**ono**

finire (-isc-): _to finish_

io	fin**isco**	noi	fin**iamo**
tu	fin**isci**	voi	fin**ite**
lui/lei/Lei	fin**isce**	loro	fin**iscono**

Person
Persona

Italian tenses are made up of six persons, three singular and three plural (*number*). Verbs must agree in number with the subject of your phrase.

singular	plural
io (*I*)	noi (*we*)
tu (*you*)	voi (*you*)
lui (*he*)/lei (*she*)	loro (*they*)

The pronoun **Lei** (always capitalized) also serves as a formal pronoun and is used to addresses strangers, clients, and other situations where you do not know the person well. It uses the same form as the third person singular **lei.** The pronoun **tu** is the familiar form of the pronoun *you* and is used with people you know well, such as family members, children and animals.

Esso/a or **Essi/e** are pronouns that are equivalent to the English *it* but are used mainly in writing, such as administrative documents, textbooks, and literature.

The subject pronouns in Italian are generally omitted (since the verb ending indicates the person). They are often added for emphasis or to avoid ambiguity.

Moods
Modi

In Italian, there are two moods: finite and non-finite. Finite moods are those with defined subjects. Finite moods are those tenses in the **indicativo** (*indicative*), **congiuntivo** (*subjunctive*), **imperativo** (*imperative*), and **condizionale** (*conditional*).

17

Non-finite moods are those that do not have defined subject and are the **infinito** (*infinitive*), **gerundio** (*gerund*) and **participio** (*participle*).

Tenses
Tempi

Each mood in Italian is made up of one or more tenses. The chart that follows outlines the various tenses. In Italian, there are two kinds of tenses: **semplice** and **composto** (*simple* and *compound*). Simple tenses have just one verb form. Compound tenses are comprised of an auxiliary verb (**essere** or **avere**) and a past participle (**ausiliare** e **un participio passato**).

Irregular verbs
Verbi irregolari

Italian has many irregular verbs. Some of them will be profiled in this book. There are too many irregular verbs to list here, but many of the most common and useful will be profiled here. Most grammar books have verb charts throughout and/or appendices that profile many irregular verbs. A good dictionary also indicates whether a verb is irregular. A useful online tool for checking verb conjugations is the web site http://www.italian-verbs.com.

Finite Moods / *modi finiti*

indicativo	congiuntivo	condizionale	imperativo
presente	presente	presente	presente
passato prossimo*	passato*	passato*	
imperfetto	imperfetto		
trapassato prossimo*	trapassato*		
passato remoto			
trapassato remoto*			
futuro semplice			
futuro anteriore*			

Non-finite moods / *modi infiniti*

infinito	gerundio	participio
semplice	semplice	semplice
composto*	composto*	composto*

*compound tense / **tempo composto**

NB: Remember that **il condizionale** is not a *tense,* but a *mood* made up of two tenses: **presente** and **passato**. It is important when talking about tenses (like **il presente**) that you clarify the mood, since there are four *present tenses*: **indicativo, congiuntivo, condizionale** and **imperativo.** This book will not explore every single tense or mood in depth, but the names of most of the tenses are provided here as a point of reference. All of the examples used throughout the book make use of almost all of the tenses listed above.

Verbs to know

Whether you are a beginner or an advanced student of the language, the following verbs should be memorized in all tenses and moods. These are verbs that are used frequently and in a variety of grammatical situations. You should know them by heart and be able to use them with ease.

For a complete conjugation on all of the verbs profiled in this chapter, consult a dictionary, a grammar book or use an online tool, such as http://www.italian-verbs.com.

avere
to have

Avere, along with **essere**, is one of the most important verbs in Italian. Not only do **avere** and **essere** figure in a number of common and useful everyday expressions, but both verbs function as auxiliaries in compound tenses. **Avere** means *to have* in English, but it is used in many Italian expressions where you would say "I am..." in English, such as saying how old you are (**quanti anni hai?**). Another example can be seen below in the expression, **avere paura**:

> Da piccolo non **ho** mai **avuto paura** del buio.
>
> *As a child, **I was** never **afraid** of the dark.*

dare
to give

Dare means *to give* and is an important verb in Italian. It is also used in a variety of expressions, as in the example below (**dare per scontato qualcosa**). Note that it is irregular in the present tense:

20

> Non bisogna mai **dare** per scontata un'amicizia,
> perché può finire dall'oggi al domani.
>
> *You should never **take** a friendship **for granted**, because it
> could be over from one day to the next.*

essere
to be

Like **avere**, **essere** is one of the most important verbs that
every student must know backwards and forwards. Like
avere, it is also an auxiliary verb for intransitive verbs in
compound tenses and in passive constructions (**il passivo**).
It is equivalent to the English verb *to be* and is a verb that is
used in dozens of common, everyday situations:

> Nella vita **è** davvero importante essere sempre se
> stessi!
>
> *In life **it is** really important to always be yourself.*

fare
to do, to make

Fare means *to make* or *to do* but also has other meanings
depending on the context. It is used in a variety of
expressions (**fare una festa** / *to throw a party*) and can be
used with another infinitive to convey the idea of having
someone do something (**Ho fatto preparare un bel
pranzo** / *I had a good lunch prepared*):

21

> Non sarà facile riparare al grave danno che **hai fatto** alla società.
>
> *It will not be easy to atone for the grave damage **you did** to society.*

piacere
to like

Piacere is a verb that confuses many English speakers who are learning Italian because the verb *to like* in English is *transitive*. In Italian, though, it is *intransitive*. It helps to think of **piacere** as meaning *to be pleasing to someone*; this can make the construction appear more logical. **Piacere** takes **essere** in compound tenses.

Be careful how you use this verb with liking people. **Mi piaci** means *I like you* but *not* in the *platonic* way. Also remember that the person *doing the liking* is always the indirect object of the phrase. The person or persons (or *thing* or *things*) that are being liked determine the number of the verb.

I have a friend who doesn't like fish or seafood, so when offered a meal of this type, it is not uncommon to hear him remark:

> Non **mi è** mai **piaciuto** il pesce, e mai **mi piacerà**!
>
> *I never **liked** fish, and I **will** never **like it**.*

stare
to stay, to remain

Stare is another important verb to know because it is linked to a variety of expressions. It can mean *to stay* or *to remain* but can also be used to convey how one feels or ask how someone feels. You will often hear "**Come stai?**" (*"How are you?"*) to which you might respond "**Sto bene**" (*"I'm fine"*).

Stare is also **un verbo fraseologico** (*phraseological verb*), which means it is often combined with another verb (and also a preposition) to convey a different meaning than its usual one. **Verbi fraseologici** describe the progress of an action (whether the action is imminent (as in our example below), in progress (as in our second example), continuing, or finishing):

"Ciao Federico, che fai?"

"Hi, Federico, what are you doing?"

"**Sto per andare** all'università: per caso vuoi un passaggio?"

"I am about to go to university: do you want a lift, by chance?"

As a phraseological verb, stare is also used with the **gerundio** to express actions that are in progress:

Carola non mi risponde al cellulare: probabilmente **sta riposando** e non vuole essere disturbata.

Carola is not answering my calls: she probably is resting and doesn't want to be disturbed.

23

venire
to come

Venire is another important Italian verb that is irregular in the present tense. It means *to come*, but it can also mean *to cost/to come to (a price)* (**Quanto viene?**):

> Quando un forestiero **viene** al Sud piange due volte: quando arriva e quando parte.
>
> *When a foreigner **comes** to the South he cries twice: when he arrives and when he leaves.*

Attenzione: Venire is also used to form the passive (for simple tenses only) with the past participle.

Verbs For Daily Activities

When learning Italian, it is important to learn *useful verbs* that can help you to describe things that you do every day, such as *waking up, sleeping, eating,* and *getting dressed.* Since we all have unique and varying lives, it is impossible to list every single verb that might describe our daily activities. As you learn a new language, try to make it a point to learn verbs that will help you to convey these daily rituals. The verb profiled in this section highlight some common activities that almost all of us are bound to do regularly.

alzarsi
to get up

Alzarsi means *to get up* from the bed, but it can also mean *to stand up*, depending on the context. When I was a child, my mom was always frustrated because I would never wake up after my alarm went off. She would often say:

> Ogni mattina è la stessa storia: mio figlio **non si alza** dal letto nemmeno con le bombe!
>
> *Every morning it is the same story: my son **doesn't get out** of bed even with bombs!*

chiamarsi
to be called

Chiamarsi is an important reflexive verb to know and means *to be called.* We use this verb when we introduce ourselves or say who someone is, such as the new exchange student from Germany who joined our class:

> Ho appena saputo che domani avremo in classe un nuovo compagno: a quanto pare **si chiama** Franz e viene da Berlino.
>
> *I just found out that tomorrow we will have a new student in class: it seems **his name is** Franz, and he comes from Berlin.*

fare colazione
to make breakfast

Fare colazione means *to have breakfast*. Note the absence of the definite article. Living in Italy, you get used to eating a simple breakfast of coffee and a couple of cookies or biscuits. If I skip breakfast and do not have my *cappuccino* and *cornetto* in the morning, my day gets off to a bad start:

> È vero quando si dice che la giornata comincia storta se **non si è fatta colazione**: non a caso è uno dei pasti più importanti.
>
> *It is true when they say your day will be off if you don't have breakfast: it is not by chance that it is one of the most important meals.*

fare/farsi la doccia
to take a shower

Fare/farsi la doccia means *to take/to have one's shower*. We all have that friend who always has to be clean or cannot go anywhere without having a good shower first, like our friend, Clara:

> Clara è una maniaca dell'igiene personale: **si fa la doccia** ben tre volte al giorno.
>
> *Clara is obsessive about personal hygiene: **she takes a shower** as much as three times a day.*

giocare (a)
to play

Giocare (a) means *to play*. The simple preposition **a** *always* precedes the game being played:

> Tra i tanti passatempi della mia infanzia, il mio preferito era **giocare a** nascondino.
>
> *Among the many hobbies of my childhood, my favorite was playing hide-and-seek.*

mettere la sveglia
to set the alarm

Mettere la sveglia (or **impostare la sveglia**) means *to set the alarm,* a common every day habit that many of us are bound to do to avoid oversleeping. I personally find travel a bit stressful, so I am the type loves to get to the airport or train station with plenty of time to spare:

> Prima di andare a dormire devo ricordare di **mettere la sveglia** intorno alle 6 del mattino, così avrò tre ore di tempo prima della partenza.
>
> *Before going to sleep, I have to remember **to set the alarm** for around about 6 AM so I will have three hours before departing.*

stirare
to iron

Stirare means *to iron,* and it is one of my *least favorite* everyday activities. The word for *iron* in Italian is **il ferro (da stiro)**.

When I was a child, my mom would pull out the ironing board and press everyone's shirts and pants for the week on the weekend. It was not a great time to hang around the house, and each of us always found something else to do while my mom would iron our clothes:

> Povera mamma: oggi **ha stirato** tanti di quei vestiti che ha riempito quasi tutta la stanza!
>
> *Poor mom: today **she ironed** so many of these clothes that she almost filled up the whole room!*

svegliarsi
to wake up

Svegliarsi means *to wake up*. This is the point in which your eyes open, and you are no longer sleeping. It does not necessary mean you have gotten out of bed. It only means that you are awake (**sveglio/a**).

I used to have a job working in a call center and would need to wake up very early five to six days a week. Being on time was very important!

> Per poter arrivare puntuale in ufficio sono costretto a **svegliarmi** ogni giorno alle 5: che stress!
>
> *In order to be able to get to work on time, I have **to wake up** every day at 5 AM: what a strain!*

togliersi i vestiti
to undress, to take off one's clothes

Togliersi i vestiti means *to undress* or *to take off one's clothes*. It is more common than the verb, **svestirsi**, which has a more figurative usage.

Imagine it is an extremely hot day, and you are at a wedding and dressed to the nines. You are feeling uncomfortable in the hot July weather! You might remark:

> Oggi fa un caldo infernale! Non vedo l'ora di arrivare a casa e di **togliermi i vestiti!**
>
> *Today it is as hot as hell! I can't wait to get home and **take off my clothes**!*

telefonare
to phone, to telephone

Telefonare means *to phone* or *to telephone.*

In Italian, you **telefonare <u>a</u> qualcuno** or **a un numero** (*to phone a number*). Do not forget the preposition because **telefonare** is *intransitive* in Italian!

The other day I finally received my credit card from the bank here in Italy, but it would not work. I complained to my friend:

> **Ho** più volte **telefonato** al centro assistenza per l'attivazione della mia carta di credito, ma ancora non funziona.
>
> *I phoned customer support again and again to activate my credit card, but it still doesn't work.*

vestirsi
to get dressed

Vestirsi means *to get dressed.* This is something all of us do every day. Everyone has a friend (or perhaps it is you?) who never knows what to wear for any given occasion, such as my friend Mario:

> Siamo alle solite: anche questa volta Mario **si è vestito** in modo non appropriato al contesto.
>
> *Here we go again: also this time Mario **dressed** inappropriately for the occasion.*

Irregular or Notable Verbs

These five verbs profiled below are notable because they are irregular or have a particular usage.

riuscire (a)
to succeed, to manage, to be able to, can

Riuscire (a) means *to manage* or *to succeed* in doing something. A common mistake many students of Italian make is to confuse this verb with **potere** (see the next section on modal verbs):

> Benché fosse malato, **è riuscito a** portare a termine il suo lavoro: è un uomo davvero eccezionale!
>
> *Even though he was sick, **he managed to finish his work**: he is really an extraordinary guy.*

(Non) riuscire a is used when we have made an attempt to do something but for some reason, we cannot *manage* to make the action happen (or *are unable to* or simply *can't*):

> **Non riesco ad** aprire la porta: la maniglia sembra essersi rotta!
>
> *I **can't** open the door: the handle seems to have broken.*

sentire
to hear, to feel, to smell

Sentire is a verb of perception that can be translated a couple of different ways, like when we are listening to the radio and *hear* some important news:

> **Ho sentito** alla radio che chiuderanno
> definitivamente il centro storico al traffico: era ora!
>
> *I heard on the radio they will definitely close the historic
> downtown to traffic: it's about time!*

Or when we are waiting to go to the doctor's office for our
annual flu vaccination and do not want *to feel* any pain from
the needle:

> Più tardi andrò a fare il vaccino antinfluenzale: ho
> una paura matta dell'ago, nonostante mi abbiano più
> volte rassicurato che **non sentirò** alcun dolore.
>
> *I will go get the flu shot later: I am deathly afraid of needles,
> even though they reassured me over and over again **I will
> not feel** any pain.*

Sentire can mean *to hear*, *to feel something* and even *to smell*.
Like **vedere**, **sentire** can also be used with infinitives, such
as: **Ho sentito cadere qualcosa in cucina** / *I heard
something fall in the kitchen.*

tenere
to keep, to take

Tenere can mean *to keep* or *to take something*. This verb
features in many idiomatic expressions. Note that it is also
irregular in the present tense (**tengo, tieni, tiene,
teniamo, tenete, tengono**). Imagine you are driving and
need *to keep* to your lane:

31

> Quando guidi in strada, è importante che tu **tenga** sempre la destra per evitare di invadere la corsia opposta.
>
> *When you driving on the road, it is important that you always **keep** right to avoid encroaching on the opposite lane.*

The verb can also be used when you want one of your friends to take a book you are handing to him because it might help them do better when he retakes his exam:

> Ecco, **tieni** questo libro: leggerlo ti aiuterà a riflettere sugli errori che hai commesso.
>
> *Here, **take** this book: read it because it will help you to reflect on the mistakes you made.*

uscire
to go out, to leave

Uscire means *to go out*. It can also mean *to leave* when used with the prepositions **di** or **da** with locations, such as **uscire di casa/di fabbrica/di prigione** (*to leave home/to leave the factory/to get out of prison*) or **uscire dal carcere/ cinema/teatro** or **dallo stadio**, etc. (*to get out of prison/to leave the movies/to leave the theater/to leave the stadium*).

Imagine that you are preparing for an important exam, and you have been cooped up in the house for days and days. You might say to a friend:

Per via degli esami sono stato costretto a rimanere chiuso in casa: non vedo l'ora di **uscire** e di rilassarmi!

*Because of exams, I was forced to stay closed up at home: I can't wait **to go out** and relax!*

Modal Verbs

Italian has three verbs that are considered **modal verbs** or **verbi modali/servili.** These verbs are **dovere, potere,** and **volere**. The verb, **sapere**, also has a *servile* function and will also be examined. The four verbs combine with other infinitives, but they can also be used autonomously. We will look at each one and see how its meaning or use changes when used autonomously (**Voglio un cane**) or as a modal (**Devo andare al supermercato**).

dovere
to have to, must
to owe

Dovere means *to have to* or *must* when used as a modal. Yesterday, you missed your friend Giulia's birthday party because you weren't feeling well and had to go to the emergency room. A friend of yours calls you up to see what happened:

> "Perché ieri non sei andato al compleanno di Giulia?"
>
> *"Why didn't you go to Julia's birthday yesterday?"*
>
> "**Sono dovuto** andare al pronto soccorso perché ho avuto forti giramenti di testa e senso di nausea."
>
> *"I had to go to the emergency room because I was very dizzy and nauseous."*

When used autonomously, it means *to owe*. Your friend, Paolo, lent you some money a few nights ago when you went out for beers, and now you would like to pay him back:

> "Paolo, quanti soldi ti **devo**?"
>
> *"Paolo, how much money do **I owe** you?"*
>
> "Mi devi 10€, ma non preoccuparti: non c'è alcuna fretta!"
>
> *"You owe me 10 euro, but don't worry: there's no rush!"*

potere
to be able to, can

Potere means *to be able to* or *can*. When used as a modal verb, it is used to make requests, express possibilities or impossibilities (in the negative) or convey having an ability to do something. Domenico, Claudio's roommate, wants to know if his friend is free tomorrow night given that it's Friday night, and they have both been studying all week. Unfortunately, it is impossible:

> "Claudio, domani sera ti va di andare a cenare fuori?"
>
> *"Claudio, do you feel like going out to eat tomorrow evening?"*
>
> "Mi piacerebbe tanto, ma **non posso** uscire! C'è il compleanno di mia madre e ci rimarrebbe male se non ci fossi."
>
> *"I would really like to, but **I can't** go out! There is my mother's birthday, and she would be disappointed if I wasn't there."*

As an autonomous verb, it often translates as *can* when the infinitive is implied or easily discernible from the context of the phrase without being explicitly stated:

> Claudia e Tommaso non facevano altro che litigare: ho fatto tutto quel che **potevo** (fare) per riappacificarli, ma hanno deciso di lasciarsi.
>
> *Claudia and Tommaso used to do nothing but argue: I did everything that **I could** (do) to bring them together, but they decided to break up.*

volere
to want

Volere, as a modal, means *to want to do something* when there is a desire. This verb should not be confused with **potere**, which, especially in questions and queries, expresses a possibility. **Volere** expresses desires or wants. Poor Enrico is doing his chemistry homework and has, unfortunately, no appetite while he labors away over his chemical formulae:

> "Enrico, **vuoi cenare** adesso o più tardi?"
>
> *"Enrico, **do you want to eat dinner** now or later?"*
>
> "Mamma, preferirei mangiare tra un po', così finisco di fare i compiti."
>
> *"Mom, I would prefer to eat in a bit, so I can finish doing my homework."*

As an autonomous verb, **volere** means *to want something*. Your friend Sara and her mother are shopping for school clothes, and her mother spots a shirt she knows her daughter will love:

> "Sara, quale maglietta ti piace? Quella rossa o quella rosa?"
>
> *"Sara, which shirt do you like? The red one or the pink one?"*
>
> "**Voglio** quella rosa: è davvero carina!"
>
> *"I want that pink one: it is really cute!"*

sapere
to know, to know how to (+ infinitive)

Sapere *is not* a modal verb by nature, but it has the ability to become one when followed by the infinitive. As a modal, it means *to know how to do something* and is often also translated as *can*. Imagine that you are walking around the small Italian town of Palestrina. You cannot find your mobile phone in your bag, and you do not have a watch. You pop into a nearby bar to ask the barista for the time:

> "Scusa, **sai dirmi** per caso che ore sono?"
>
> *"Pardon, can you tell me by chance what time it is?"*
>
> "Certo, sono le tre del pomeriggio proprio adesso."
>
> *"Of course, right now it is three o'clock in the afternoon."*

As an autonomous verb, it means *to know* a fact or knowledge. Think about the last exam you took where you knew the answer to every question and aced it:

> Ho superato l'esame! **Sapevo** tutte le risposte e per
> questo ho ricevuto un bel voto!
>
> *I passed the exam!* ***I knew*** *all the answers, and for this
> reason I got a good grade!*

Be careful not to confuse **sapere** with **conoscere**.
Conoscere means *to know someone or something* in the sense
of being familiar with someone or something:

> **Conosci** il nuovo disco dei *Coldplay*? È mitico!
>
> ***Do you know*** *the new Coldplay CD? It is fantastic!*

Some specific rules govern which auxiliary is used in compound tenses as well as the placement of pronouns. Let's recap:

1. In compound tenses, the auxiliary is determined by the infinitive which follows the modal. If the modal is followed by a verb that takes, **avere**, then **avere** is used in compound tenses. If the modal is followed by a verb that takes **essere**, then **essere** is used:

    Non **sono dovuto andare** all'università oggi.
    Today, I didn't have to go to university.

    Ho potuto finalmente **comprare** quella roba al supermercato.
    I was finally able to buy that stuff today at the supermarket.

2. If the infinitive, **essere,** follows the modal, **avere** is used:

    Maria **ha voluto essere** sincera con noi.
    Maria wanted to be sincere with us.

3. If the infinitive which follows the modal is passive, **avere** is used:

    Quella macchina **ha dovuto essere comprata** da Gianna.
    That car must be bought by Gianna.

4. If the atonal pronouns **mi, ti, si, ci,** or **vi** (as reflexive pronouns) come before the modal, **essere** is used. If they attach to the infinitive, **avere** is used:

    Si sono dovuti dire addio prima della partenza.
    Hanno dovuto dir**si** addio prima della partenza.

    They had to say good-bye to each other before the departure.

Pronominal Verbs

Pronominal verbs (**verbi pronominali**) are verbs that use one or more particles (such as **la, se, ne** and **ci** or some combination) to create a verb that has its own meaning that is often distinct from the original verb (**andarsene** v. **andare**, for example). This section will look at some of the most common pronominal verbs.

andarsene
to go (away), to take off

Andarsene means *to go* but is more emphatic. It is often translated as *to go away*, especially when used in the imperative (**Vattene** / *Go away*). This form of **andare** adds a layer of emotion, urgency, or some other emotive quality.

Imagine you are the head of an office in Rome. You are looking for one of your employees, Davide, who has to give an important presentation in the morning. You run into Clara in the hallway. Perhaps she knows where he is?

> "Ciao Clara! Ho bisogno di parlare con Davide: sai dirmi, per caso, dove posso trovarlo?"
>
> *"Ciao, Clara! I need to talk with Davide: Can you tell me, by chance, where I can find him?"*
>
> "Non lo troverai qui in ufficio: **se n'è appena andato** via!"
>
> *"You will not find him here in the office: **he just took off!**"*

> ***Da notare!*** *In compound tenses with **essere**, the past participle agrees in gender and in number with the subject of the sentence.*

andare + pronome indiretto
to feel like

Andare + pronome indiretto (*indirect object pronoun*) is a common way of expressing a desire in Italian and is synonymous with the expression **avere voglia di.** This construction is very common, and you will hear it used often.

The latest action film has just come out, and you are dying to see it. No one seems to be interested in the film, but you know your friend, Marco, is always up for a fast-paced action flick! You give him a call on your mobile:

> "Marco, **ti va** di andare al cinema?"
>
> *"Marco, do you feel like going to the cinema?"*
>
> "No, oggi non **mi va** affatto!»"
>
> *"No, I don't feel like it at all today."*

Da notare! *Remember that this construction with* **andare** *is an indirect one: the subject of your phrase is <u>not</u> the person who is doing the desiring but the thing being desired (which also determines the number of the verb)!*

averci
to have

Averci is the pronominal form of the verb **avere.** It has the same meaning as **avere** (*to have*) but is more colloquial. Although it is often considered a form used most often in the center and south of Italy, you will hear it used all over Italy. It is almost exclusively a spoken phenomenon. In formal writing its usage should be avoided.

Imagine that you are at your friend Paolo's home. You walk by a bookshelf in his room, and you remember that you lent him your history book a few months ago. You have an exam coming up, and you would like it back:

> Paolo, per caso **ci hai** tu il mio libro di storia?
>
> *Paolo, **do you have** my history book by chance?*

Note that the particle, **ci**, does not elide (or merge) with the conjugated form of **avere** when written even if, when spoken, it is not always heard (**c'hai** = **sbagliato!**)

avercela (con qualcuno)
to be mad (at someone)
to have it in (for someone)

Avercela means *to be mad (at someone)* or *to have it in (for someone)*. This is a verb that you will hear as you are traveling around Italy, especially if you are able to understand conversations that are going on around you. One time on the metro in Rome, I was sitting next to two teenagers. I was traveling from the Battistini station all the way to Re di Roma, and I caught this bit of their conversation:

> Da giorni Teresa si comporta in modo alquanto strano nei miei confronti: **ce l'ha con me**, forse?
>
> *Teresa has been behaving quite strangely towards me: perhaps **she is mad at me**?*

cavarsela
to get by, to make do, to know one's way around something

Cavarsela is another verb you will hear often. In Italian, it has several different but similar meanings. It can mean *to get by* or *to make do*. With the preposition, **con**, it can mean *to know one's way around something*, for example: *You really know*

42

your way around computers. / **Te la cavi proprio bene con i pc.**

I will always remember advice that my Italian teacher gave me when I first arrived in Italy, telling me:

> Non si può sempre fare affidamento sugli altri: nella vita è importante imparare a **cavarsela** da soli!
>
> *You can't always trust others: in life it is important to learn to get by on your own!*

entrarci
to fit
to have to do with

The verb, **entrarci**, has two meanings. The first translates as *to fit*. Imagine that you are packing for a vacation, and you have stuffed everything imaginable inside. Your girlfriend comes back into the bedroom with a couple of sweaters, and you remark:

> La valigia sta scoppiando: **non c'entra** nient'altro!
>
> *The suitcase is bursting: nothing else will fit!*

It can also mean *to have to do with* someone/something.:

> Mia madre è stata accusata ingiustamente dalle sue colleghe: **non c'entra nulla** con quel che è accaduto l'altro giorno!
>
> *My mom has been unjustly accused by her coworkers: it has nothing to do with what happened the other day!*

farcela

to manage; in the negative, *to be unable to go on with something*

Farcela is a pronominal verb that you will hear a lot once you get to know some native speakers! In the negative, it often translates as [*Dammit*], *I can't go on with this anymore*. It is used to express moments of extreme frustration. It can also mean *to manage,* especially when the odds were against you.

Imagine you are working on a final project that you will have to present for your course in international law! It is complicated and difficult and is taking forever to get everything organized. After studying for days, the deadline nears. You might exclaim:

> Sono a pezzi e, nonostante tutto, sono ancora a metà del lavoro... **non ce la faccio** più!
>
> *I am beat, and, in spite of everything, I am only half-done...* **I can't go on with this** *anymore!*

Farcela is also synonymous with **(non) riuscirci/riuscire (a)**. You are helping a friend move, but he has put way too much into his boxes. One of them is just too heavy for you:

> **Non ce la faccio** (*or* **non riesco**) a tenere questa scatola ancora per molto: è troppo pesante!
>
> *I am unable to carry this box for much longer: it is too heavy!*

(non) fregarsene
to not give a damn
to not give a squat

(Non) fregarsene is an important verb to know because, in spite of what any Italian will tell you, everyone uses it, and you will hear it a lot.

The best equivalent in English might be *to not give a damn* or *to not give a squat*. Be careful how you use this expression as it is a bit on the strong side. The adverb, **niente**, is often added for emphasis and follows the verb.

I have a friend, Danilo, who is a person of strong character who never spends much time worrying about what others think of him. We often say that:

> Danilo è una persona decisa e forte: **non gliene frega niente di** quel che gli altri pensano di lui!
>
> *Danilo is a strong and determined person: he doesn't care at all about what others think about him.*

prendersela
to get work up

Prendersela means *to get worked up* about something. Think of poor Pietro who is always the butt of practical jokes. His friends played another one on him the other day, and he is beside himself with anger. One of Pietro's friends asks what happened, and a friend responds:

> Pietro **se l'è presa** per lo scherzo che gli hanno combinato l'altro giorno!
>
> *Pietro got worked up over the joke that they played on him the other day!*

volerci
to get work up

Volerci is the pronominal form of **volere**. It means *to need* or *to take*. It is often used with expressions of time (**Ci vogliono due minuti** / *It takes two minutes*) but can also be used to convey a necessity that is often implied (especially when one talks about *money, time*, or *a great effort* that has been made.)

Think about a number of sacrifices that you have made to achieve a goal. You might say to yourself:

> Dopo tanti sacrifici, **ci vuole** proprio una bella ricompensa!
>
> *After many sacrifices, a good reward is really needed.*

Da notare!

When pronominal verbs are used in compound tenses, the past participle *might not* behave as you might think!

For pronominal verbs that end in **-la** or **-sela**, the past participle will agree with the pronoun, **la (farsela = fatta)**.

For pronominal verbs that end in **-le**, the past participle will agree with the pronoun, **le (prenderle = prese)**.

For pronominal verbs that end in **-ne**, the past participle will agree take the feminine plural form (**darne = date**).

For pronominal verbs that end in **-sene, -sela,** and **-cisi** take **essere** in compound tenses. The past participle agrees in gender and number with the subject.

Da notare!   "No Future in Time"

In English, the future tense cannot be used with certain time expressions: in other words, there are "no future in time clauses"!

Take for example the following phrase in English:

*When the package **arrives**, I **will sign** for it.*

In English, clauses that begin with *when, while, before, after, by the time, as soon as, if,* or *unless* are always followed by the present tense. In these situations, where English uses the present, Italian uses the future in both the dependent clause (that begins with a time expression) and independent clause:

Quando **arriverà** il pacco, lo **firmerò**.

When the package arrives, I will sign for it.

Also, consider the conjunction **se**:

*If I **save** enough money, I **will buy** a new car.*

In Italian, you would write:

Se **risparmierò** abbastanza soldi, mi **comprerò** una nuova macchina.

This is an excellent case where translating *word for word* will create problems for your Italian. Knowing where Italian and English grammar diverge will help you to be a better communicator in both your writing and speaking.

Da notare!   Passive Voice

The passive voice (**la voce passiva** or **il passivo**) can be formed:

• with the verb, **essere, + past participle + (da*):**

Active: Michele aveva lanciato la palla.
Actie: *Michele had thrown the ball.*

Passive: La palla **è stata lanciata da** Michele.
Passive: *The ball had been thrown by Michele.*

• with the verb, **venire,** but *only derived from simple tenses* (**tempi semplici**) **+ past participle** + (da)**

Active: Mariella mangia le mele.
Active: *Mariella is eating the apples.*

Passive: Le mele **vengono mangiate da** Mariella.
Passive: *The apples are being eaten by Mariella.*

• to express that something *should be done*, **andare + past participle** (**dovere + esssere + past participle****):

Active: Dovete pulire la stanza tre volte alla settimana.

Passive: La stanza deve essere pulita da voi tre volte alla settimana.
Passive: La stanza **va pulita da** voi tre volte alla settimana.
Passive: *The room should be cleaned by you three times a week.*

- with **si passivante*** (verb agrees with the subject):

Spesso si comprano i vestiti solo durante i saldi.

Often one buys clothes only during sales.
People often buy clothes during sales.

Remember that **si passivante** constructions cannot take an agent!

- with the modals: **dovere, potere** or **volere + essere + past participle** + (da)**

Active: Devi sgridarli quando arrivano.
Active: You have to scold them when they arrive.

Passive: **Devono essere sgridati da te** quando arrivano.
Passive: They have to be scolded by you when they arrive.

Active: Il notaio può firmare l'assegno.
Active: The notary can sign the check.

Passive: **L'assegno può essere firmato dal** notaio.
Passive: The check can be signed by the notary.

Active: I nostri compagni di squadra vogliono Claudia come capitano.
Active: Our teammates want Claudia as captain.

Passive: **Claudia è voluta dai** nostri compagni di squadra come capitano.
Passive: Claudia is wanted by our teammates as captain.

*all passive constructions *except* the **si passivante** can have an agent introduced by **da**
**past participles agree in gender & number with the subject

Palermo: Teatro Massimo (2014)

2 Nouns
Sostantivi

Nouns (i sostantivi), along with verbs, are one of the most important parts of speech in both English and Italian. In Italian, there are two kinds of nouns:

- common nouns (**nomi comuni**), which are made up of three subtypes:

    1. concrete (**concreti**): words that indicate things we can see and touch (**la macchina, il cane, la mela**)

    2. abstract (**astratti**) : words that indicate abstractions, feelings and states of being (**la speranza, la pace, il dovere**, etc.)

    3. collective (**collettivi**) : words that indicate a multitude of people or things even when used as singular nouns (such as **la gente, la polizia, il fogliame**, etc.)

- proper nouns (**nomi propri**) : nouns that refer to specific people, places or things that require a capital letter (**gli Stati Uniti, Roma, l'Asia, Napoli**)

Common nouns in Italian can be classified into four types:

1. simple (**semplici** or **primitivi**) : this is the simplest form of noun from which the other forms below are derived:

latte	*milk*	musica	*music*
posto	*place, seat*		

2. derived (**derivati**) : these nouns contain a prefix (**prefisso**) or suffix (**suffisso**) that change the meaning of the derived noun:

latticini	*dairy*	musicista	*musician*
avamposto	*outpost*		

3. altered (**alterati**) : this group of nouns are "changed" and are broken down into four sub-categories:

a. diminutive (**diminuitivo**) : by adding **-ino, -etto, -ello, -icciolo, -icino**, or **-icello** to the noun to indicate something smaller:

gatto	*cat*	gatt**ino**	*kitten*
scolaro	*pupil*	scolar**etto**	*naive person*
secchio	*bucket*	secchi**ello**	*small bucket*
porto	*port*	port**icciolo**	*marina*
libro	*book*	libr**icino**	*booklet*
vento	*wind*	vent**icello**	*breeze*

b. endearment or affection (**vezzeggiativo**): by adding **-otto, -uccio** or **-olo** to convey affection:

ragazzo	*guy*	ragazz**otto**	*strong boy*
tesoro	*treasure*	tesor**uccio***	*treasure*
figlio	*son*	figli**olo***	*son*

*these altered forms convey more affection than their simple/primitive counterparts

c. augmentative (**accrescitivo**) : by adding **-one, -accione** to indicate something that is bigger or larger:

pancia	*stomach*	panci**one**	*pot belly*
uomo	*man*	om**accione***	*hulk*

*note the change in the root to **om-**

d. pejorative (**peggiorativo**) : by adding **-accio, -ucolo, -iciattolo**, or **-astro** to indicate something derogatory or disparaging:

mostro	*monster*	mostr**iciattolo**	*little monster*
carattere	*character*	caratter**accio**	*temperamental person*
cantante	*singer*	cantant**ucolo**	*poseur*
fratello	*brother*	fratell**astro**	*step-brother*

4. compound (**composti**) : a combination of two words, such as other nouns, adjective or various forms of the verb:

n. + n.	boccaporto	*hatchway*
n. + adj.	terracotta	*earthenware*
adj. + adj.	pianoforte	*piano*
adj. + n.	biancospino	*hawthorn*
v. + adv.	posapiano*	*slowpoke*
adv. + adj.	sempreverde	*evergreen*
v. + v.	saliscendi**	*latch, ups & downs*
v. + n.	tergicristallo***	*windshield wiper*

* *from the verb, posare*
** *from the verbs, salire & scendere*
****from the verb, tergere & the noun, cristallo*

Gender
Genere

Stai attento!
The words **maschile** and **femminile** describe *gender*.

Do not confuse them with **maschio** and **femmina**!

In Italian, nouns can be either masculine (**maschile**) or feminine (**femminile**).

In general, *nouns* that are *masculine*:

- end in **-o**: dollar**o**, libr**o**, tett**o**

- end in **-ma** (from Greek): il geno**ma**, il glauco**ma**, il mag**ma**

- sometimes end with a consonant: ba**r**, fil**m** *but* la sta**r**, la mai**l**

In general, nouns that are feminine:

- generally end in **-a,** however, there are exceptions, such as il pilot**a**, il clim**a**, il poet**a**, l'autist**a**, etc.

- end in **-i, -tà,** and **-tù**, such as tes**i**, piet**à**, and gioven**tù** (Note that there are some masculine nouns that end in **-i**, such as the days of the week, il brindis**i**, lo sc**i**, etc.)

Lastly, nouns that end in **-e** can be either masculine or feminine. Don't forget that:

- the points of the compass are *masculine*: il Nord, il Sud, l'Ovest, l'Est

- the months are *masculine*: gennaio, febbraio, marzo, aprile, maggio, giugno, luglio, agosto, settembre, ottobre, novembre, dicembre

- the days of the week are *masculine* except for Sunday (**la** domenica): **il** lunedì, **il** martedì, **il** mercoledì, **il** giovedì, **il** venerdì, and **il** sabato

- lakes, seas, metals and chemical elements are generally masculine

- countries and rivers are generally masculine

- the sciences (**la** biologia, **la** chimica, etc.), subjects studied in school or university (**l'**archeologia, **la** filosofia, **la** sociologia), continents (**l'**Asia, **l'**Europa, **l'**Africa); most cities are feminine.

Many masculine nouns form the feminine by changing the ending (**la desinenza**) of the masculine noun from **-o** to **-a** or by changing the suffix. These nouns show the change in the endings:

- cuoc**o** becomes cuoc**a**

- ors**o** becomes ors**a**

Masculine nouns that end in **-a**, like **poeta**, add a suffix of -**essa**:

- poet**a** becomes poet**essa**

Masculine nouns that end in **-e** can change the ending to **-a** or **-essa**, depending on the noun to form the feminine:

- padron**e** becomes padron**a**

- cont**e** becomes cont**essa**

Masculine nouns that end in **-tore** add the **-trice** suffix to form the feminine:

- pesca**tore** becomes pesca**trice**

Masculine nouns that end in **-sore** add the **-itrice** suffix to form the feminine:

- cen**sore** becomes cens**itrice**

Like most rules, there are always exceptions, such as:

- profes**sore** which becomes professor**essa**

Some masculine nouns are irregular in their conversion to the feminine *but* share the same root:

- **re** becomes **re**gina

- **streg**one becomes **streg**a

- **d**io becomes **d**ea

Some nouns are considered independent (**nomi indipendenti**) because they have different roots for both masculine and feminine forms:

masculine		feminine	
frate	*monk*	suora	*nun*
fratello	*brother*	sorella	*sister*
marito	*husband*	moglie	*wife*
uomo	*man*	donna	*woman*
toro	*bull*	vacca	*cow*
padre	*father*	madre	*mother*
papà*	*dad*	mamma	*mom*

*note the accent for *dad*! il p̲a̲pa (no accent!) = pope

Another group of nouns are known as *promiscuous nouns* (**nomi promiscui**) because the gender remains either masculine or feminine and does not change. These forms refer to animals, and the adjectives **maschio** and **femmina** are used to differentiate the gender:

- il leopardo **maschio** / il leopardo **femmina**

- la iena **maschio** / la iena **femmina**

56

Some nouns are considered **false** because they share the same root, but the meaning of the word changes from masculine to the feminine:

masculine		feminine	
arc**o**	*bow, arch*	arc**a**	*Ark*
cas**o**	*case*	cas**a**	*house*
cors**o**	*class*	cors**a**	*run, race*
gamb**o**	*stem*	gamb**a**	*leg*
magli**o**	*mallet*	magli**a**	*mesh; shirt, jersey*
pann**o**	*cloth*	pann**a**	*cream*
port**o**	*port*	port**a**	*door*
tapp**o**	*cap, cork*	tapp**a**	*stage, lap*

Some nouns also change gender in the plural, being masculine in the singular and feminine in the plural, such as:

- **l'uovo** becomes **le** uov**a** (*egg/eggs*)

- **il** pai**o** becomes **le** pai**a** (*pair/pairs*)

The last group of nouns are those which are called invariable in gender (**nomi invariabili nel genere**) because:

- they have two forms, one for the singular and one for the plural: il/la cantant**e,** i/le cantant**i**

or

- they end in -**a, -cida, -iatra,** or -**ista** and share the same form in the singular *but* have separate plurals for the masculine and feminine: il/la barist**a,** i barist**i,** le barist**e**

Number
Numero

Number (**il numero**) refers to whether a noun is *singular* or *plural*. In Italian, the number of a noun can be usually be determined by its ending (**la desinenza**):

- masculine singular nouns that end in -**o** form the plural by changing the ending to -**i:**

alber**o**	alber**i**	*tree*
carr**o**	carr**i**	*cart*
decoll**o**	decoll**i**	*take-off*

- feminine singular nouns that end in -**a** form the plural by changing the ending to -**e:**

ciald**a**	ciald**e**	*wafer*
cart**a**	cart**e**	*paper*
gamb**a**	gamb**e**	*leg*

Except for **arma** and **ala** (*weapon* and *wing*) whose plurals are **armi** and **ali**, respectively.

- Masculine nouns that end in -**ca** or -**ga** change their endings to -**chi** or **ghi:**

arcidu**ca** becomes arcidu**chi**
strat**ega** becomes strat**eghi**

- Masculine nouns that end in -**io** whose accent falls at the next to last syllable form the plural by adding an -**i:**

z**io** becomes z**ii,**
legg**io** becomes legg**ii**

- Masculine nouns that end in **-io** whose accent falls elsewhere in the word (in other words, not the last or next to last syllable) form the plural by dropping the final **-o**:

princi**pio** becomes princi**pi**

Exception: il tem**pio** becomes i templ**i** (*temple/ temples*)

- Masculine nouns whose accent is on the third-to-the-last syllable (**nomi sdruccioli**) and end in **-co** or **-go** change their endings to **-ci** to **-gi**:

il m<u>a</u>ni**co,** i m<u>a</u>ni**ci**
l'asp<u>a</u>ra**go,** gli asp<u>a</u>ra**gi**

- Masculine nouns whose accent is on the next to last syllable (**un nome piano**) that ends in **-co** or **-go** change their endings to **-chi** or **-ghi**:

il mag**o,** i ma**ghi**
il fiasc**o,** i fias**chi**

- Masculine and feminine nouns that end in **-e** become **-i** in the plural:

il detergent**e,** i detergent**i**
la docent**e,** le docent**i**

- Feminine nouns that end in -**ca** or -**ga** change their endings to -**che** and -**ghe**, respectively:

barc**a** becomes bar**che**
pes**ca** becomes pes**che**
acciu**ga** becomes acciu**ghe**
bel**ga** becomes bel**ghe** (*f.*) *but* the masculine forms are bel**ga** (*sing.*) and bel**gi** (*pl.*)

- Feminine nouns that end in -**cia** and -**gia** change their endings to -**ce** or -**ge**, respectively, if a consonant precedes the ending:

man**cia** becomes man**ce**
goc**cia** becomes goc**ce**
roc**cia** becomes roc**ce**
bisboc**cia** becomes bisboc**ce**

- Feminine nouns that end in -**cia** and -**gia** change their endings to -**cie** or -**gie**, respectively, if a vowel precedes the ending:

cami**cia** becomes cami**cie**
vali**gia** becomes vali**gie**
farma**cia** becomes farma**cie**

- Foreign words are invariable if the word is commonly used in Italian. However, if the word is rarely used in Italian, then the foreign plural in the original language can be used.

Double plurals
Nomi sovrabbondanti

Some nouns in Italian have two plural forms. The masculine plural often indicates an abstract or subjective meaning while the feminine plural refers to the more concrete or objective meaning. This is not a hard and fast rule:

singular	masculine plural	translation	feminine plural	translation
braccio	bracci	*branches, offshoots*	braccia	*arms*
cervello	cervelli (*figurative*, fuga dei cervelli = brain drain)	*brains*	cervella	*brains (gray matter)*
fuso	fusi	*spindles*	fusa	*purring*
ginocchio	ginocchi	*knees (of one's pants)*	ginocchia	*knees (anatomical)*
labbro	labbri	*brims*	labbra	*lips*
membro	membri	*members (male sex organ)*	membra	*limbs*
osso	ossi	*bones (of butchered animals)*	ossa	*bones (of the human skeleton)*
urlo	urli	*howls (from an animal)*	urla	*screams (of a person)*

Some nouns also have double singulars and plurals, such as frutto and frutta which become frutti and frutta or orecchio and orecchia which become orecchi and orecchie. The meanings for both pairs are the same (*fruit/fruits, ear/ears*). Note that **l'orecchia** is no longer used in standard Italian.

Invariable nouns
Nomi invariabili

In the previous section, we looked at nouns that were invariable in gender. In this section, we will look at some rules that govern the invariability of the number, in other words, the **singular** and **plural** forms of the noun are identical (only the definite/indefinite article or adjective endings change).

Nouns that are *invariable in number* are:

- those masculine nouns that end in **-a**: il sos**a** (*look-alike*)**,** il vagli**a** (*money order*)

- feminine nouns that end in **-o**: la dinam**o**, l'ec**o**, la libid**o**

- nouns which have an accented last syllable: il caff**è**

- nouns which end in consonants (mainly foreign words): il fil**m**, il ba**r**

- nouns which have only one syllable: il **re**, lo **sci**, la **gru**

- truncated nouns (la bic**i**/le bic**i**, la mot**o**/le mot**o**)

- certain colors (**blu, rosa, viola**)

- feminine nouns which end in **-ie** (except for mogl**ie**, superfic**ie**, effig**ie**): la calviz**ie** (*baldness*), la ser**ie** (*series*), la progen**ie** (*offspring*)

Defective nouns
Nomi difettivi

Italian also has a class of nouns that are *defective*, in other words: they only have a singular form or only a plural form.

The following singular nouns are considered *defective*:

- nouns that indicate a collection of people or things, such as la **gente** (*people*), il **fogliame** (*foliage*)

- abstract nouns: la **fame** (*hunger*), la **sete** (*thirst*)

- diseases: il **morbillo** (*measles*)**,** la **scarlattina** (*scarlet fever*)

- names of metals and chemicals: il **titanio** (*titanium*)**,** l'**ossigeno** (*oxygen*)

- non-count nouns (**nomi non numerabili**): il **latte** (*milk*), la **neve** (*snow*), il **sangue** (*blood*)

The following plural nouns are considered *defective*:

- nouns in the plural that indicate a variety or multiplicity: i viver**i** (*provisions*), i dintorn**i** (*surroundings*)

- nouns of learned origins: le feri**e** (*vacation, holidays*), le calend**e** (*calends*), i poster**i** (*posterity*), le nozz**e** (*wedding*)

- nouns in the plural that refer to compound objects, such as: le **redini** (*reins*)

Nouns
Sostantivi

By increasing your vocabulary, you can move away from describing things that you are unfamiliar with as **quella cosa** or **questa roba**. The nouns highlighted here are words I have encountered and learned since my arrival here in Italy. They are useful to know, and many of them combine with certain verbs and expressions.

The best way to build your vocabulary is by reading newspapers, magazine articles, books and surfing Italian web sites. Try to use the context provided as you are reading to determine the meaning of new words. As you get more proficient, move away from bilingual dictionaries to a good monolingual Italian dictionary.

l'agio
ease (at ease)

This is a useful noun to know in Italian, and it is one that you will hear often if you listen carefully. It is often used with the verbs **essere** (**a proprio agio**) or **sentirsi** (**a proprio agio**) to mean *to be/to feel at ease/comfortable*. It can also be used with the verb, **mettere** (**qualcuno a proprio agio**) to mean *to make someone feel comfortable* or *to put someone at ease*:

> Non mi sono mai sentito **a mio agio** nell'ufficio dove lavoro.
>
> *I never felt at ease in the office where I work.*

It can also be used with the verb, **vivere** (**vivere tra/negli agi**) to mean *to live in comfort* or *luxury*:

> Dopo **aver vissuto** per anni **tra gli agi**, a Clelia verrà difficile abituarsi ad uno stile di vita più sobrio e povero.
>
> *After having lived for years in comfort, Clelia will find it difficult to get used to a more sober and poor lifestyle.*

il botto (di)
a ton of

The noun **il botto** literally means *knock* or *shot*. However, it is more commonly used with the indefinite article, **un botto (di)**, to mean *a boatload* or *a ton of* something (synonymous with **un sacco di, tanto**). It is more colloquial than **un sacco di**:

> Non andrò più in quel ristorante: mi hanno fatto pagare **un botto di** soldi!
>
> *I will not go to that restaurant anymore: they made me pay a boatload of money!*

It is also common to see this noun in the expression, **in un botto**, which means *in no time* or *in one go*:

> Nonostante fosse gremita di gente, la piazza si svuotò **in un botto** appena cominciò a piovere.
>
> *Even though it was elbow to elbow with people, the piazza emptied in no time as soon as it started raining.*

il casino
mess, disorder, racket

Stai attento!

The word for casino (where you gamble) is **il casinò** (*m. & inv.*).

Il casino (without the accent!) can also mean *whorehouse* or *brothel*!

Il casino is a common noun that you will hear living in any big Italian city, which is full of problems: incessant noise, traffic jams, crowds of tourists at museums and restaurants! It is more often used with the indefinite article **un**:

> I ragazzi del piano di sopra hanno fatto **un casino** insopportabile ieri sera, con quella musica ad alto volume!
>
> *The kids who live one floor up made **a racket** yesterday evening with that music turned all the way up!*

Another noun with a similar meaning is the word, **il macello**. It literally means *slaughterhouse*, but, in Italian, it often means *disaster* or *shambles*. Like **un casino**, it is used with the indefinite article. Both expressions are more or less interchangeable, even if **un macello** refers more to "spatial" disasters than to those caused by sounds or clamor:

> La stanza di mio figlio è **un macello**: i libri e i vestiti sono sparsi dappertutto!
>
> *My son's room is **a disaster**: books and clothes are scattered everywhere!*

il chicco
grain, kernel

Il chicco means *grain* or *kernel*. The word for rice in Italian is **riso**, but, like in English, we do not say: *I put rices in the pan*. You would say *I put some grains of rice in the pain*. The same goes for *coffee*: a coffee bean = **un chicco di caffè**.

A single grape would be **un acino d'uva**!

> Nessuno penserebbe mai che quel gioiello, poco più grande di **un chicco**, possa valere così tanti soldi!
>
> *No one ever would have thought that jewel, no bigger than **a grain**, could be worth so much money!*

il conservante
preservative

Il conservante means *preservative,* in other words, those chemicals that go into our food to preserve them and keep them from going bad (**marcio**).

I do not list this word because I am a proponent of **conservanti**. This word creates *so many problems* for students of Italian because it is a *false friend*! Remember that **il preservativo** means *condom*! Be careful how you use this word: believe me, using it wrong can lead to some hilarious consequences!

> Questa panna da cucina è senza **conservanti**, per cui deve essere consumata nell'arco di qualche giorno dall'apertura della confezione.
>
> *This cooking cream has no **preservatives**, therefore it has to be used within a few days of opening the container.*

il dispositivo
device, equipment

If you have traveled by air throughout Italy as often as I have, you are bound to hear this word on your flights when the flight attendant asks you to turn off your electronic devices, **i dispositivi elettronici**.

> Ho installato un sistema all'avanguardia per la protezione domestica: per attivarlo basta servirsi di **un dispositivo** di accensione a distanza.
>
> *I installed a security system to protect the house: in order to turn it on, all you have to do is use the remote activator.*

la fila
line, queue

The word **la fila** means *line* or *queue*. If there is one thing that people in Italy dislike doing, it is waiting in line for something! You can also use the word, **la coda**. Let me tell you: one place that I can't stand waiting in line here in Italy is at the supermarket:

> Oggi al supermercato, c'era davvero tanta gente: ad ogni cassa c'era da fare **una fila** incredibile!
>
> *Today at the supermarket, there were just so many people: at every cash register there were people waiting in long **lines**!*

la manciata
handful

La manciata means *handful* or, in some contexts, *a bit*. It is almost always used with the indefinite article, **una.** Don't forget that this is considered a *quantity* (in Italian, it is called **una quantità ridotta**, like **un sorso** / *sip,* **un bicchiere** / *cup,* etc.): when you use it with the indefinite article on its own, you need to make to include the pronoun **ne**!

> Ha speso così tanto per l'acquisto della casa che adesso è rimasto con **una manciata** di soldi.
>
> *He spent so much buying the house that he now has only a **bit** of money left.*

> Di solito, quando ho fame, mi piace mangiare delle noci: ne prenderò giusto **una manciata** così da sentirmi sazio fino alla cena.
>
> *Usually, when I am hungry, I like to eat some nuts: I will take only a **handful** so that I feel satisfied until dinner.*

il mocio
mop

The word **il mocio** means *mop*. You won't find it in any dictionary: it is the brand name of a mop manufactured in Germany for the Italian market that has entered the Italian language! I remember the first time I heard it. My friend had spilled something on the floor and asked me to get the **mocio** from the bathroom. *"The what?"* I asked! I have never heard the mop called anything else but **il mocio** here in Italy!

> Ho chiesto alla mia coinquilina di passare **il mocio** in cucina, ma come al solito ha rimandato le pulizie a chissà quando.
>
> *I asked my roommate to **mop** the kitchen, but, as usual, she put off cleaning until who knows when.*

la pillola
pill

La pillola is the Italian word for *pill*, such as aspirin or other medicine. Don't confuse it with the word **la pasticca**: in the plural **le pasticche** often refer to illegal drugs like ecstasy.

The expression **indorare la pillola** means *to sugarcoat something* or *to sugar the pill*:

> Pur avendo aumentato le tasse considerevolmente, il governo ha cercato di **indorare la pillola** elargendo dei bonus per le famiglie meno abbienti.
>
> *After having increased taxes considerably, the government tried **to sugarcoat** it by giving bonuses to less well-off families.*

il segnalibro
bookmark

The word **il segnalibro** means *bookmark*. It is the indicator or placeholder that we put in our books to save the page we are on. This word in Italian can also be used for the same *bookmarks* we save on our computer for web sites and other useful web pages (even if the words **i bookmark** or **i preferiti** are also common when talking about the computer):

> Nel riordinare la mia camera, mia madre ha fatto cadere per terra il romanzo che iniziai a leggere qualche giorno fa, facendo scivolare via **il segnalibro**: dannazione, a che pagina ero arrivato?
>
> *While reorganizing my room, my mother dropped the book I started reading a few days ago fall, causing the **bookmark** to fall out: dammit, what page was I on?*

il soffitto
ceiling

The ceiling in the house is **il soffitto**:

> Più volte, quando sono a letto, mi capita di fissare per minuti **il soffitto** e di non riuscire a prendere sonno.
>
> *Very often when I am in bed, I end up staring at the ceiling for several minutes and am unable to fall asleep.*

The word **il tetto** means *roof* of the house, but it can also be used figuratively to refer to the *ceiling* or *limit* of something, such as the *income ceiling* or a *ceiling on spending*, and so forth:

> Ho fissato **un tetto** massimo per le spese mensili per evitare sprechi non desiderati.
>
> *I set a maximum limit for monthly expenses to avoid undesirable waste.*

lo strofinaccio
dish/tea towel

In Italian, there are several words for *dish/tea towel*, and **lo strofinaccio** is one of them (along with **il canovaccio**). There are several words in various dialects that you might encounter, too, but these two words here should cover you!

> Ho passato energicamente **lo strofinaccio** sul tavolo, ma non c'è stato verso di eliminare quella macchia.
>
> *I energetically passed the dish towel along the table, but there was no way to get rid of that stain.*

il termosifone
heater, radiator

Il termosifone means *heater* or *radiator*. I included the noun here because I had the hardest time remembering how to pronounce it. Now I love the way it sounds! It is also a useful word to know since the radiators can leak at times, and, if you need to call a plumber, you will be better able to explain the problem!

> In questa casa c'è un freddo insopportabile: purtroppo la caldaia si è guastata e non posso accendere **i termosifoni**!
>
> *At home it is unbearably cold: unfortunately, the water heater broke, and I can't turn on **the radiators**!*

la zanzariera
screen

La zanzariera is *the screen* we put in windows to allow the air inside but keeps the bugs outside! In Italian, the word is similar to the noun **la zanzara**, which means *mosquito*. It can also mean *mosquito net* for those nettings put over beds at night to keep the bugs away:

> Grazie alla **zanzariera** che ho fatto montare in camera, ho potuto dormire tranquillamente con le finestre aperte, senza essere punto dalle zanzare.
>
> *Thanks to the **mosquito net** I had installed in the room, I was able to sleep peacefully with the windows open without being bitten by mosquitoes.*

3 Article
Articolo

The article (**l'articolo**) is considered one of the most important parts of speech in Italian because it is so frequently used.

In English, our articles are *a/an* and *the*. In Italian, the definite and indefinite article change to accommodate the gender and number of the noun that it precedes. While English has three articles to learn, Italian has eleven!

The definite article in Italian (**l'articolo determinativo**) is the equivalent to the English *the*. The indefinite article, (**l'articolo indeterminativo**) is the equivalent to the English *a* or *an*.

Italian also has the partitive (**l'articolo partitivo**) that is used to express *some of a larger group* and is considered the plural of the *indefinite article*. In Italian, the partitive is formed with the articulated forms of the preposition, **di**, as shown here.

del
dello
della
dei
degli
delle

Definite article
Articolo determinativo

The definite article in Italian must agree in gender and in number with the noun that it precedes:

masculine				feminine		
singular		plural		singular	plural
il	lo (l')*	gli	i	la (l')*	le

l' is the elision of **lo or **la** when they precede a noun that begins with a vowel.*

Here are some rules that govern the definite article in Italian:

- If the masculine noun starts with a **s + consonant**, **pn**, **gn**, **z** or **y** then **lo** is used:

  lo gnocco
  lo zaino

- If the masculine noun starts with a vowel, then **lo** elides with the vowel that follows and becomes **l'** -- this is obligatory:

  l'arco
  l'orrizonte

  Lo is used before nouns beginning with the letter *i* or *j + vowel* because of the semi-consonant sound: **lo** Ionio

- **Il** comes before nouns beginning with all other consonants:

  il carro
  il tetto

- **Gli** is the masculine plural form for **lo (l')**:

  lo scopo, **gli** scopi
  l'arco, **gli** archi

- Nouns that employ **il** as the definite article use **i** in the plural:

  il mattone - **i** mattoni
  il bidone - **i** bidoni

- For feminine nouns that begin with a vowel, **la** elides with the vowel that follows and becomes **l'** (this is obligatory in Italian). For feminine nouns that start with a consonant, **la** is used:

  l'ombra
  la macchina

  La does not elide with nouns beginning with the semi-consonant sound of *i* or *j* + *vowel*: **la iena** (*hyena*)

- For feminine nouns, **le** is the plural. **Le** never elides:

  le ombre **but never** l'ombre
  le macchine

- If an adjective comes between the noun and the definite article, the article matches the gender and number of the noun *but* the first letter of the adjective determines the final choice of definite article:

  l'anatra *but* **la povera** anatra
  gli uccelli *but* **i maledetti** uccelli
  lo sportello *but* **il sesto** sportello

Uses of the definite article
Usi dell'articolo determinativo

The definite article has some special uses that we will outline below. It is important to know the correct use of the definite article because, by modifying it, we can give different meanings to a phrase or discourse. Take for example this phrase:

> Ho visto **la** parata
>
> *I saw the parade.*

This phrase means that you saw a specific parade that the listener (or reader) would presumably know. Now consider:

> Ho visto **una** parata
>
> *I saw a parade.*

This phrase means that you attended some parade that might have been going on at the moment and does not refer to a specific parade.

The meaning of a phrase can also be determined by the presence of the article or by its absence. Take the phrase:

> Francesco è **un** musicista.
>
> *Francesco is a musician.*

This phrase means that Francesco is *one of many musicians* that exists or musicians I know belongs to this category. If we said:

Francesco è **il** musicista.

Francesco is the musician.

This phrase means that Francesco is that particular musician that was talked about and whose work and style we know well. Or perhaps he has done something important or particular? But if we say:

Francesco è musicista.

Francesco is (makes a living as) a musician.

This phrase means that Francesco practices music as his profession or as his hobby. Note the absence of the definite and indefinite article.

The definite article (**l'articolo determinativo**) is used:

- in front of important works of art, literature, etc:

Hai letto **il** *Decameron* di Bocaccio?

Have you read Bocaccio's Decameron?

But when we want to refer to a general work by a particular artist or writer, we use the *indefinite article* (**l'articolo indeterminativo**):

Ho visto **un** Monet all'esposizione.

I saw a Monet at the exhibit.
(in other words, a painting by Monet)

- in front of names of some newspapers and periodicals:

> Non leggo mai **il** Corriere della Sera.
>
> *I never read the Corriere della Sera.*

- in front of nicknames:

> Lo chimano Fausto **il** Grande.
>
> *They call him Faust the Great.*

- in front of the last names of women or in front of last names in the plural:

> Ti piace come recita **la** Lopez?
>
> *Do you like how Ms. Lopez acts?*

> **I** Leto sono una famiglia perbene.
>
> *The Leto's are a respectable family.*

- in front of geographical names, such as the names of regions, seas, large islands, states, mountains, lakes, and rivers:

lo Ionico, **la** Puglia, **l'**Italia, **il** Vesuvio, **la** Senna, **il** lago di Como

- When the definite articles precede the days of the week, it means that some action occurs habitually:

> **La** domenica andiamo in chiesa.
>
> *Every Sunday we go to church.*
> *On Sundays we go to church.*

- The definite article can be placed before other parts of speech to create nouns:

> **Il** sapere è potere.
>
> *Knowledge is power.*

> **I** rossi sono **i** miei preferiti.
>
> *The red ones are my favorites.*

> Prendo sempre **il** meglio dalla vita!
>
> *I always take the best from life!*

The definite article **is not used**:

- when we refer to indefinite quantities:

> Hanno acquistato **piatti** e **posate** per la festa.
>
> *They purchased plates and cutlery for the party.*

- when we refer to an imprecise element:

> Agì con **parsimonia** ed **eleganza**.
>
> *He acted parsimoniously and elegantly.*

- with certain expressions, such as:

avere fretta *to be in a hurry*
avere fame *to be hungry*
perdere tempo *to waste time*
dare retta *to pay attention/listen to someone*
cambiare idea *to change one's mind*
sentire caldo/freddo *to feel hot/cold*

- in front of proper names of people (**il** Francesco, **la** Monica). In the North of Italy, however, *it is common* when referring to people in the third person to place the definite article in front of the last names of famous or illustrious individuals:

> **Verdi** (*not* il Verdi) fu uno degli operisti più acclamati nella storia della musica italiana.
>
> *Verdi was one of the most acclaimed opera composers in the history of Italian music.*

- in front of the names of cities (Palermo, Roma, Parigi) *but* **Il** Cairo, **L'**Aquila, **La** Spezia

Indefinite article
Articolo indeterminativo

The indefinite article (**articolo indeterminativo**) in Italian is the English equivalent to *a* or *an*. In Italian, it is used to refer to something generic and not yet determined.

In Italian, the indefinite article has the following forms:

masculine		feminine
un	uno	una (un')

- The masculine indefinite article, **uno**, is used before nouns that begin with **s + consontant, ps-, gn-, y,** and **z**:

uno zio   **uno** gnocco
uno psicologo   **uno** yogurt

- **Un** is used for all masculine nouns beginning with vowels and other consonants:

un albero   **un** carciofo

Attenzione: a common mistake to use the **un'** form with *masculine* nouns: this form of the indefinite article is reserved only for feminine nouns that start with a vowel.

- **Una** elides, becoming **un'**, before feminine nouns beginning with a vowel:

un'anatra   **un'**idiota

- **Una** is used before all other feminine nouns that begin with consonants:

una macchina   **una** penna

Partitive
Partitivo

The partitive is a way of expressing *some* part of a whole. In English, for example, we might say: *I would like some potato chips.* In Italian, this form is often considered the plural of the indefinite article. There are several ways of expressing the partitive in Italian.

With the preposition, di:

The articulated forms of the preposition, **di**, can be used to express the partitive. The forms can be seen in the chart below:

articulated forms of the preposition, di	definite article
del	**il**
dello	**lo**
della	**la**
dei	**i**
degli	**gli**
delle	**le**

Note that the plural forms of the articulated preposition are the plural forms of the indefinite article whereas the singular forms are used to express a generic quantity of something. Let us look at some examples in action:

Puoi darmi **delle** patatine?

*Can you give me **some** chips?*

Il mio professore mi ha dato **dei** compiti complicati!

*My teacher gave me **some** complicated homework!*

The partitive with the preposition **di** is generally avoided:

1. in other prepositional phrases since **di** + **articolo** is already a prepositional phrase:

> Sono andato con **degli** amici al concerto!
>
> **Better**:
> Sono andato **con** amici al concerto.
>
> *I went with some friends to the concert.*

2. in negative phrases:

> Non ho uova a sufficienza per la ricetta.
> (Non ho **delle** uova per la ricetta) **wrong**!
>
> *I do not have enough eggs for the recipe.*

3. if the noun is preceded by an quantity adjective or by a phrase that describes the material the noun is made of:

> In genere mangio **molta** verdura.
>
> *In general I eat **a lot** of vegetables.*

> Ho bisogno di 200 grammi **di burro**.
>
> *I need 200 grams **of butter**.*

4. with lists of things:

> Quando vai in cartoleria, compra **colla, carta** e **buste per lettere.**
>
> *When you go to the stationer's, buy glue, paper and letter envelopes.*

> In piazza c'erano **turisti, ragazzi del posto,** e **venditori ambulanti.**
>
> *In the square there were tourists, locals, and pedlars.*

5. as the first word of the sentence:

> **Degli** amici mi hanno portato all'aeroporto.
>
> **Better:**
> **Alcuni amici** mi hanno portato all'aeroporto.
>
> *Some friends brought me to the airport.*

6. in certain fixed expressions, such as avere caldo/fame/sete/sonno, provare pietà, prendere fiato, etc.

With alcuni/alcune and qualche:

The partitive can also be expressed using the indefinite adjectives, **alcuni/alcune** (remembering that it is used in the plural and agrees in gender with the noun it modifies) and **qualche** (remembering that it is used only in the singular):

> Lo spettacolo in piazza è stato organizzato da **alcuni ragazzi** del quartiere.
>
> *The show in the square was organized by **some guys** in the neighborhood.*

> Hai per caso **qualche spicciolo** da darmi?
>
> *Do you have by chance **any change** to give me?*

With no partitive, using the noun in the plural:

The partitive can also be expressed using the plural noun by itself with no modifiers:

> "Mamma, ho visto **ombre spaventose** muoversi nella mia stanza!"
>
> *"Mamma, I saw **some scary shadows** moving in my room!"*
>
> "Daniele, avrai avuto **incubi**! Torna a letto!"
>
> *"Daniele, you will have had **some nightmares**! Go back to bed!"*

4 Adjectives
Aggettivi

Adjectives in Italian function as specifiers, adding detail and characteristics to the nouns they modify. In Italian, they also agree in gender and number with the noun they are modifying.

Adjectives in Italian have two functions:

- attributive (**attributivo**) : this is when the noun and adjective are directly connected to each other. In Italian, it generally implies proximity: **la mela rossa**

- predicate (**predicativo**) : just like in English, the adjective can be a predicate. This happens only with helping verbs (**le copule**), such as **essere, sembrare, parere, restare, rimanere, risultare, diventare, nascere, morire,** etc.

Adjectives of both classes can be either *descriptive* (**qualificativi**) or *determiners* (**determinativi**). We'll look at both types in the following pages.

Descriptive adjectives
Aggettivi qualificativi

Descriptive adjectives (**aggettivi qualificativi**) are those adjectives that describe qualities or characteristics of a person or thing. There are three classes of **aggettivi qualificativi:**

1. first class (**la prima classe**): these are adjectives that have four different endings (**le desinenze**) depending on the gender and number of the noun being modified:

masculine		feminine	
singular	plural	singular	plural
ross**o**	ross**i**	ross**a**	ross**e**

2. second class (**la seconda classe**): these are adjectives that have two endings depending only on the number of the noun being modified:

masculine & feminine	
singular	plural
interessant**e**	interessant**i**

3. third class (**la terza classe**): these are adjectives that end in **-ista, -asta, -cida,** and **-ita.** They have three endings: one ending for both singular masculine and feminine nouns, and two separate plural forms depending on the gender of the noun being modified:

masculine & feminine	masculine	feminine
singular	plural	plural
entusiast**a**	entusiast**i**	entusiast**e**

There is a final group of adjectives that are *invariable* (**invariabili**). These adjective do not change form and remain the same regardless of the gender or number of the noun being modified. The following adjectives are typically invariable:

1. adjectives that end in an accented vowel or end in a consonant, for example: zul**ù**, sno**b**

2. adjectives that end in the letter, **-i**, for example: par**i**, dispar**i**

3. adjectives that indicate a color when the adjective is derived from the noun, for example: **blu, rosa**. When color adjectives (*varaible* and *invariable*) combine with other adjectives (*not only the invariable ones*) or nouns, all the adjectives/nouns in the group also become invariable: **degli abiti verde scuro** / *some dark green clothes*; **dei guanti verde menta** / *some mint green gloves*

4. adjectives that start with the prefix, **anti-**, for example: **anti**uomo, **anti**nebbia

Adjectives can also be used comparatively. In Italian, there are five types of comparisons, called *degrees* (**gradi**):

1. **grado positivo**: this *degree* simply expresses the characteristic without any comparison.

2. **grado comparativo di maggioranza**: this degree expresses superiority, for example, saying that something or someone has more of a quality than another person or thing. This is conveyed using the expression, **più + aggettivo + di/che:**

Marco è **più** tollerante di me.

*Marco is **more** tolerant than me.*

3. **grado comparativo di uguaglianza**: in this degree, there is a balance between the qualities compared; in other words, no one person or thing is greater or worse than the other. This construction can be formed with the adverbs, **così** (only in negative constructions) and **come,** or with **tanto** and **quanto**, which must agree in gender and number when they modify nouns:

Marco non è (**così**) tollerante **come/quanto** me.

*Marco is not **as** tolerant **as** I am.*

Giovanni ha **tanta** pazienza **quanta** ne ha Marco.

*Giovanni has **as much** patience **as** Marco.*

4. **grado comparativo di minoranza**: this degree expresses inferiority and is expressed using the expression, **meno + aggettivo + di/che**:

Marco è **meno** tollerante di me.

*Marco is **less** tolerant than me.*

5. **grado superlativo**: this degree expresses the maximum of any given quality expressed by the adjective or the minimum and is divided into two sub-groups:

a. relative (**relativo**) : the relative superlative communicates the most or least amount of a quality of one person or thing against a group of people or things. It is formed using **the definite article + più** *or* **meno + adjective + di**:

> Annalisa è **la meno patetica dei** miei amici.
>
> *Annalisa is **the least pathetic of** my friends.*

> La Bibbia è **il libro più letto dei** testi religiosi.
>
> *The Bible is **the most read book** of religious texts.*

b. absolute (**assoluto**): the absolute superlative expresses the maximum quality possessed by a person or thing without any comparison. The absolute form is formed by adding the following suffixes (as always, they vary based on the gender and number of the noun the adjective modifies):

singular		plural	
masculine	feminine	masculine	feminine
-issimo	**-issima**	**-issimi**	**-issime**

Francesco è **simpaticissimo**.

Francesco is very very nice.
or
Francesco is extremely nice.

The absolute superlative can also be expressed:

1. by using the the first degree adjective (**il grado positivo**) with adverbs, such as **assai, davvero, molto, decisamente**:

Marco è stato **davvero maleducato**.

Marco was really rude.

2. by repeating the adjective:

> Sono entrati in casa **piano piano**.
>
> *They entered the house **very quietly**.*

3. by adding prefixes, such as **arci-**, **stra-**, **extra-**, **sopra-**, **sovra-**, **ultra-**, to the adjective of the 1st degree:

> La mia camera è **ultramoderna** quanto a mobilia.
>
> *My room is **ultramodern** due to the furnishings.*

4. by adding another adjective of the first degree after the first adjective -- this second adjective would have a meaning similar to the first one:

> Sono appena uscito dall'ufficio e sono **stanco morto**.
>
> *I just left the office and am **dead tired**.*

5. by adding **tutto** in front of the adjective of the first degree (making sure that **tutto** agrees with the noun being modified):

> Sara era **tutta spaventata** all'idea di prendere l'aereo.
>
> *Sara was **totally scared** of the idea of taking the airplane.*

Da notare!   Comparisons of inequality

Comparisons of inequality can be expressed in Italian by **più di/che (grado di maggioranza)** or with **meno di/che (grado di minoranza)**. How do you know when to use **di** or when to use **che**?

Use the preposition, **di**:

- when you are comparing *two* people or things against *one* quality:

  Marco è più intelligente **di** Andrea.
  *Marco is more intelligent **than** Andrea.*

- when numbers are involved in the comparisons:

  Marco pesa meno **di** 65 kg!
  *Marco weights more **than** 65 kg!*

Use **che**:

- when you are comparing two different qualities against *one* person or thing, remembering that the quality can be an adjective but not only:

  Marco è meno fortunato **che** determinato.
  *Marco is less fortunate **than** determined.*

- when the comparison involves prepositional phrases:

  Marco è incline più al lavoro individuale **che** alla collaborazione.
  *Marco is more keen on working alone **than** in groups.*

- when there are infinitives:

  Preferisco più stare a casa **che** uscire in giro per locali.
  *I prefer staying at home more **than** going out to bars.*

Irregular comparatives & absolute superlatives

Comparativi irregolari & superlativi assoluti irregolari

The adjectives **buono, cattivo, grande**, **piccolo, alto,** and **basso** have irregular comparatives and superlatives as do **molto** and **poco**.

The chart below shows the comparatives and superlatives for the adjectives mentioned above. These forms should be memorized since making comparisons between people and things is a common activity in any language. Understanding how to use them and remembering to use them properly will add *color* and *depth* to your Italian:

positive		comparative		superlative	
buono	*good*	**migliore**	*better*	**ottimo**	*best*
cattivo	*bad*	**peggiore**	*worse*	**pessimo**	*worst*
grande	*big*	**maggiore**	*bigger*	**massimo**	*biggest*
piccolo	*small*	**minore**	*smaller*	**minimo**	*smallest*
alto	*tall*	**superiore**	*taller*	**supremo**	*tallest*
basso	*short*	**inferiore**	*shorter*	**infimo**	*shortest*
molto	*a lot*	**più**	*more*		
poco	*little*	**meno**	*less*		

The comparative forms can also be combined with the adverb, **più**, such as **più buono, più cattivo,** etc. The superlative forms can also be made using **-issimo/a/i/e: buonissimo, cattivissimo,** etc. Both the regular and irregular forms are correct:

> Questo dolce è **più buono** di quello dell'altra volta.
> Questo dolce è **migliore** di quello dell'altra volta.
>
> *This dessert is **better** than the last time.*

Avviso! Some adjectives do not have a comparative or a superlative, especially those adjectives that describe shapes, such as **rotondo, triangolare, quadrato, rettangolare,** etc.). For example, in Italian, one *cannot* say:

> Quella cosa è **più rotonda della** mia. **wrong!**
>
> *That thing is rounder than mine.*

Other adjectives also fall into this category, such as **preferito**. Something is either your *favorite* or it isn't; it is already superlative and cannot be enhanced any further!

Determiners
Aggettivi determinativi

Determiners (**aggettivi determinativi**) are adjectives that, as their name suggests, *determine* a particular reference: in other words, possession, quantity (definite or indefinite), or closeness. This section will look at five **aggettivi determinativi**:

1. possessive adjectives (**aggettivi possessivi**)

2. demonstrative adjectives (**aggettivi dimostrativi**)

3. indefinite adjectives (**aggettivi indefiniti**)

4. interrogative adjectives (**aggettivi interrogativi**), which, like the pronouns, can also be exclamative (**esclamativi**)

5. cardinal and ordinal numbers (**aggettivi numerali, cardinali** o **ordinali**)

Possessive adjectives
Aggettivi possessivi

Possessive adjectives (**aggettivi possessivi**) indicate ownership or possession. They can also function as pronouns (see chapter 5). They are almost always used with the definite article and come before the noun (although there are exceptions, see the exceptions on the next page):

masculine		feminine	
il mio	i miei	la mia	le mie
il tuo	i tuoi	la tua	le tue
il suo	i suoi	la sua	le sue
il nostro	i nostri	la nostra	le nostre
il vostro	i vostri	la vostra	le vostre
il loro	i loro	la loro	le loro

Possessive adjectives agree in gender and number with the nouns they modify, *not* with the possessor! The possessor, however, determines *what* possessive to use. For example:

> (**Io**) ho fatto tardi all'appuntamento, perché non trovavo **le mie chiavi** di casa.
>
> *I was late to the meeting because I couldn't find **my house keys**.*

The possessive adjective of the first person is chosen because the keys belong to the possessor, **io**. The form, **mie**, is chosen because the noun, **la chiave**, is feminine and in the plural (**chiavi**).

This becomes more important when our phrase is in the third person singular or plural:

Marco ha fatto tardi all'appuntamento perché non trovava **le sue chiavi di casa.**

Marco was late to the appointment because he couldn't find his house keys.

Nota bene!
Possessive adjectives almost *always* precede the noun they modify.

However, there are some idiomatic expressions and exclamations which place the possessive *after* the noun:

a modo mio
in my own way

in cuor mio
in my heart of hearts

i cazzi suoi
his f*cking business

The possessive, **suo,** and its variants mean *his/her* or *yours* (formal & capitalized: **Suo**). When the possessor is plural, you must use **il/la/i/le + loro**:

Marco e Gina hanno fatto tardi all'appuntamento, perché non trovavano **le loro chiavi di casa.**

Marco and Gina were late to the appointment because they couldn't find their house keys.

Be careful when using possessives in certain constructions. For example, when the possessors in your phrase are ambiguous. For example, take the the following phrases:

Marco ha dato appuntamento a Marta sotto **casa sua.**

Alfredo ha chiesto a Danilo se desiderava usare **la sua moto.**

Maria ha detto a Luca che **il suo comportamento** è stato inadeguato.

In those phrases, the ownership is unclear. Whose house? Marco's or Marta's? Whose motorcycle? Alfredo's or Danilo's? Whose behavior? Maria's or Luca's? In order to make the phrase clearer and avoid ambiguity, substitute the possessive adjective with a **complemento di specificazione** (genitive) or with the use of **proprio**:

> Marco ha dato appuntamento a Marta sotto **casa sua.**
>
> *Marco met Marta outside [his? her?] house.*
>
> **Notice that we aren't sure *whose* house! Let's qualify our examples:**
>
> ... sotto **casa propria** (cioè di Marco).
> *... outside his house (in other words, Marco's house).*
>
> ...sotto casa **di lei** (cioè di Marta).
> *...outside her house (in other words, Marta's house).*
>
> ...sotto casa **di un'altra persona.**
> *...outside someone else's house.*

In general, the **possessive adjective** should be preceded by the definite article. In Italian, the definite article is dropped:

- with members of the family: **padre, madre, figlio, figlia, marito, moglie, fratello, sorella, nonno, nonna, nipote, cugino, cugina, zio, zia,** etc.

However, the definite article *is used* when the family member's name is *altered*. For example: **il mio fratellino, la sua figliaccia**, etc.

The definite article is also used when the family member's name is modified by another adjective or when there is a **complemento di specificazione**:

La mia povera mamma piange sempre quando passa davanti ad un cimitero!

My depressed mother always cries when she passes by a cemetery.

Il mio cugino di Domodossola arriva lunedì.

My cousin from Domodossola arrives Monday.

Demonstrative adjectives
Aggettivi dimostrativi

Demonstrative adjectives are **quello** (*that*), **questo** (*this*) and **codesto** (*this*). **Quello** and its variants refer to someone or something distant from the speaker, while **questo** refers to someone or something that is close. **Codesto** can refer to people or things that are close to the speaker/reader.

The forms of **quello** are similar in form to the definite article (the adjective, **bello**, follows the same pattern). Their forms can be seen below:

	masculine				feminine	
quello*	quello	quel	quei	quegli	quella	quelle
questo*	questo		questi		questa	queste
codesto	codesto		codesti		codesta	codeste

* **Quell'** can be used for masculine and feminine nouns beginning with a vowel: **quell'albero; quell'arancia**. Also, **questo** and **questa** can drop their final vowel in front of nouns beginning with a vowel, but it is not required: **questa aura** or **quest'aura**

Indefinite adjectives
Aggettivi indefiniti

Indefinite adjectives (**gli aggettivi indefiniti**) are those adjectives that describe people or things generically. They are divided into three categories: **invariabili** (*invariable indefinites*) and **variabili nel genere** (*gender variable indefinites*) and **variabili nel genere e nel numero** (*gender and number variable indefinites*).

The first two categories are used only with singular nouns. *Gender variable indefinite adjectives* agree with the gender of the singular noun they modify.

100

invariable indefinite adjectives:

ogni, qualche, qualsiasi

> **Ogni** volta che andiamo al cinema, c'è sempre qualcuno che chiacchiera durante il film!
>
> *Every time I go to the movies, there is always someone who chats during the film!*

gender variable indefinite adjectives:

nessuno, ciascuno

> Non voglio **nessun** problema al lavoro.
>
> *I don't want **any** problems at work.*

Attenzione!

Many indefinite adjectives are singular in Italian but translate as plurals in English!

gender and number variable indefinite adjectives:

alcuno, certo

> **Certe** persone non sanno comportarsi in pubblico!
>
> *Certain people do not know how to behave in public!*
>
> **Alcuni** amici vanno in Spagna per Ferragosto.
>
> *Some friends are going to Spain for Ferragosto.*

Interrogative adjectives
Aggettivi interrogativi (e escalamativi)

Interrogative adjectives (**aggettivi interrogativi**) are divided into the same categories as indefinite adjectives.

The adjective, **che** (*what, which*), is invariable, while **quale** (*what, which*) is variable only in number. **Quanto** is variable in both gender in number.

Che and **quale** are used in questions when we want to know the identity or quality of something:

> **Che** film vorresti vedere stasera?
>
> *What film would you like to see tonight?*
>
> **Quale** libro stai comprando?
>
> *Which book are you buying?*

Quale *does not elide* with the verb, **essere**:

> **correct**: **Qual** è il tuo film preferito?
>
> **incorrect**: **Qual'è** il tuo numero di cellulare?
>
> *What is your mobile phone number?*

Quanto is used to ask the quantity of something:

> **Quanto** costa il cappuccino?
>
> *How much is the cappuccino?*

Cardinal and ordinal numbers

Numeri cardinali e ordinali

Just as with English, Italian has two kinds of numbers, cardinal (**numeri cardinali**) and ordinal (**numeri ordinali**). Cardinal numbers are the natural numbers that we use to count things or for mathematics:

> Mia madre mi ha comprato **tre** camicie al centro commerciale.
>
> *My mom bought me **three** shirts at the mall.*

Ordinal numbers indicate a succession of people or things:

> Lui è il **primo** ragazzo che io abbia mai amato!
>
> *He is the **first** guy I ever loved!*

One of the main differences between the two types of numbers is the use of the definite article with ordinal numbers. Generally, the definite article does not precede nouns modified by cardinal numbers. Cardinal and ordinal numbers almost always precede the noun they modify:

> "Quanti cornetti desidera?"
>
> *"How many croissants would you like?"*
>
> "Ne vorrei **due** e un caffè americano, per favore."
>
> *"I'll take **two** of them and a caffè americano!"*

> "Il **sesto** senso" è uno dei miei film preferiti!
>
> *The **Sixth** Sense is one of my favorite films.*

ordinal numbers (numeri ordinali)	
1st	primo
2nd	secondo
3rd	terzo
4th	quarto
5th	quinto
6th	sesto
7th	settimo
8th	ottavo
9th	nono
10th	decimo

There are some rules to remember when using numbers, and we will profile them here:

1. Compound numbers, such as **ventritré, sessantatré**, that end in **tre** should have an accent on the final -**é**.

2. **Venti**, **trenta**, and so on drop the final vowel before adding -**uno** and -**otto**: **ventuno, ventotto, trentuno, trentotto, quarantuno, quarantotto**

3. Note that the numbers **cento** and **mille** do not drop the final vowel when adding -**uno** or -**otto**: **centouno, centootto, milleuno, milleotto**; *However,* **cento** *does* drop the final -**o** when used with **ottanta**: cent**ottanta,** duecent**ottanta**, etc.

4. In Italian, the decimal point or period (.) is used as a decimal separator, whereas in English the comma is used:

   2,508 = two thousand five hundred eight = 2.508

5. You will often see the decimal separator eliminated and a space used in its place: this is often seen in newspapers and magazines and only when the number is *five digits or more*:

   50.000 = cinquantamila = **50 000**
   4.000 = quattromila = **4000**

6. In Italian, the comma (,) is used to indicate decimal places, whereas in English the decimal point is used:

cardinal numbers (numeri cardinali)			
1	uno	26	ventisei
2	due	27	ventisette
3	tre	28	ventotto
4	quattro	29	ventinove
5	cinque	30	trenta
6	sei	40	quaranta
7	sette	50	cinquanta
8	otto	60	sessanta
9	nove	70	settanta
10	dieci	80	ottanta
11	undici	90	novanta
12	dodici	100	cento
13	tredici	200	duecento
14	quattordici	300	trecento
15	quindici	1.000	mille
16	sedici	2.000	duemila
17	diciassette	10.000	diecimila
18	diciotto	100.000	centomila
19	diciannove	1.000.000	(un) milione
20	venti	1.000.000.000	(un) miliardo
21	ventuno		
22	ventidue		
23	ventitré		
24	ventiquattro		
25	venticinque		

4.58 = four point five eight = 4,58

7. The definite article, **il**, or its articulated variants (**del, dal, nel,** etc.) come before the year:

> **Nel 2012** sono andato a vivere in Italia.
>
> *In 2012 I went to live in Italy.*

8. When expressing days of the month, the cardinal number is used *except* for the first day of each month:

> il **primo** dicembre = December
>
> 1st *but*
>
> il **quindici** ottobre = October 15th

9. **Uno** is *not* used with the number **100** (**cento**) nor with the number **1000** (**mille**).

10. **Uno** *is used* with 1.000.000 (**un milione** / *one million*) and 1.000.000.000 (**un miliardo** / *one billion*).

11. In Italian, fractions are formed by combining cardinal numbers with ordinal numbers:

> 2/3 = two thirds = **due terzi**
>
> 1/4 = one quarter = **un quarto**

12. Italian also uses multipliers as adjective, such as **singolo, doppio, triplo, quadruplo, quintuplo** (*single, double, triple, quadruple, quintuple*, etc.).

13. Italian also abbreviates its ordinal numbers as we do in English (1st, 2nd, 3rd, 4th, and so on) with either a superscript **a, o, e** or **i**, depending on the gender of the noun it modifies:

1^a = prim**a**

1° = prim**o**

1^e = prim**e**

1^i = prim**i**

14. Ordinal numbers can also be abbreviated using Roman numerals, for example:

il **XIII** secolo = il **tredicesimo** secolo

Adjectives
Aggettivi

Learning adjectives in Italian is important because they add color, depth, and details to your speaking and writing. Since I have been living in Rome, one of the most challenging aspects of using the language every day is being able to describe things in more depth. As your Italian improves, it is important to find other ways of describing things that go beyond adjectives like **interessante** or **bello**. My Italian friends always tease me because I tend to overuse the adjective, **interessante**. It is a constant challenge to find new ways of describing people and things. Improving your ability to describe people and things with more variety is an important step in adding color and flavor to your language.

This section presents some useful descriptive adjectives I have learned in the past two years through conversation with friends or through reading. The best way to build your vocabulary is by reading books and stories. These works, tend to be more descriptive than newspapers and magazines.

angusto
narrow

The adjective **angusto** is often used to described spaces that are narrow and tight. In many Italian cities, you will often find cramped living conditions, especially in older parts of the city. It reminds me a small dwelling I once visited when I was in Catania, Sicily. My friend remarked:

> Quel poveretto è costretto a vivere in una casa dagli spazi **angusti**, con camere troppo piccole pure per un bambino.
>
> *That poor man is forced to live in a house with **narrow** spaces, with rooms too small even for a child.*

blando
mild, tame

The adjective **blando** means *mild* or *tame*. In Rome a few years ago, there were riots in the streets when the government did not fall as many had predicted. Some protests turned violent, and many of the solutions proposed by the government to deal with the city's problems were often deemed to be too mild or tame. You can imagine the mayor's adviser might have remarked:

> La soluzione che hai proposto, purtroppo, risulta essere troppo inefficace e **blanda** per sedare gli animi di quei facinorosi!
>
> *The solution that you proposed, unfortunately, ends up being too ineffective and **tame** to cool the passions of those rioters!*

borioso
haughty, arrogant

Borioso means *haughty* or *arrogant*. It is used to describe people who are just a little *too big for their britches*. In the example below, my friends, Giulia and Marco, were discussing a fellow classmate of theirs, David, while at university. Giulia remembered him but for all the wrong reasons:

> "Giulia, per caso conosci Davide?"
>
> *"Giulia, do you know David by chance?"*
>
> "Chi, quel ragazzo **borioso** ed antipatico che crede di essere un genio?!"
>
> *"Who, that **arrogant** and rude guy who thinks he is a genius?"*

109

brioso
lively, peppy

The adjective **brioso** is a playful adjective and means *lively* or *peppy*! Imagine you are walking down a crowded street in Siena where there is a group of street performers getting ready for the Palio. The performers are practicing some musical numbers to liven up the crowd during the festivities:

> In strada c'è un gruppo di musicisti che allieta i passanti con della musica **briosa** e coinvolgente.
>
> *There is a group of musicians in the street who are livening up the passersby with **lively** and engaging music.*

edulcorato
sugarcoated

The adjective **edulcorato** means *sugarcoated*, but it is also used in a figurative sense to describe something unpleasant that has its true qualities disguised:

> Quella propinatati [propinata a te] dai tuoi genitori è una visione **edulcorata** della realtà: al mondo c'è, purtroppo, molta più povertà e violenza di quella che credi!
>
> *Your parents have given you a **sugarcoated** view of reality: there is, unfortunately, a lot more poverty and violence in the world than you think!*

ennesimo
umpteenth

The adjective **ennesimo** is a useful adjective and is one that you will hear a lot in Italy. It means *umpteenth*. How many of us have older parents who are not technologically savvy? Just ask Francesco:

> Ho dovuto spiegare per **l'ennesima** volta a mia madre come funziona il suo smartphone: che stress!
>
> *I had to explain to my mother for the **umpteenth** time how her smartphone works: so stressful!*

esanime
lifeless, inert
dead

The adjective **esanime** means *lifeless* or *inert*, but it can also be a synonym for the adjective **morto** (*dead*):

> Hanno trovato stamane, sulla riva del fiume, il corpo **esanime** di una povera ragazza: sarà morta annegata, probabilmente!
>
> *This morning they found the **dead** body of a poor girl on the bank of the river: she will have probably died by drowning!*

fatiscente
crumbling, dilapidated

Fatiscente means *crumbling* or *dilapidated*. It is used to describe places that are falling apart or a bit in need of some renovation work. Imagine Carla and her mom are going around town looking for a spot to host Carla's graduation party. She and her mother can't seem to agree on anything:

> "Carla, ti piace questo locale per la tua festa?"
>
> *"Carla, do you like this place for your party?"*
>
> "Mamma, stai scherzando?! È un posto **fatiscente**... sta letteralmente cadendo a pezzi!"
>
> *"Mamma, are you kidding? It is a **dilapidated** space... it is literally falling to pieces!"*

iracondo
hot-tempered
quick-tempered

The adjective **iracondo** means *hot-* or *quick-tempered*. It is used to describe people who anger easily, like my friend, Stefano:

> Stefano si è sempre distinto per il suo carattere **iracondo**: basta poco per farlo arrabbiare.
>
> *Stefano is always known for his **quick-tempered** nature: it doesn't take much to make him angry.*

lezioso
affected, simpering, contrived

Lezioso means *affected, simpering,* or *contrived*. It is used to describe someone or something that is somewhat pretentious or artificial:

> Le frasi, a volte un po' troppo sdolcinate, del suo romanzo lo rendono uno scrittore **lezioso**.
>
> *The phrases of his novel, at times a bit too corny, make him a **simpering** writer.*

proprio
his/her/their
one's own

Proprio is a possessive adjective that almost no one ever uses correctly, even native speakers! Care must be taken when you employ this possessive. **Proprio** can:

1. function as a synonym for **suo/sua** or **loro**:

> Fausto è davvero egoista: pensa solo ed esclusivamente ai **propri** (ai suoi) **interessi**.
>
> *Fausto is really selfish: he thinks only and exclusively about **his interests**.*

2. reinforce the possession, to give the sense of *one's own* with another possessive adjective:

> Quella donna ha sacrificato **la sua propria vita** per salvare il marito!
>
> *That woman sacrificed **her own life** to save her husband!*

3. substitute for **suo/sua** in impersonal constructions (this is obligatory in Italian!):

> Bisogna sempre prendersi cura **dei propri cari** e **della propria famiglia.**
>
> *One always needs to take care **of his/her loved ones** and **his/her family.***

It is important to note that **proprio** *always* refers back to the subject of the phrase! If the noun that it modifies doesn't refer back to the subject but to another person or thing in your phrase, you must use **suo/sua** or **loro**, depending on the context and situation!

> I miei nonni hanno sempre avuto a cuore i miei genitori ed **il loro*** benessere.
>
> *My parents and **their well-being** were always dear to my grandparents' heart.*

***Il loro** is used because we are talking about the *well-being* of the *parents*, not the *grandparents*.

solerte
diligent, industrious, hard-working

Solerte means *diligent, industrious,* or *hard-working.*

> Il mio assistente è stato molto **solerte** nella conduzione del lavoro affidatogli: ha mostrato grande professionalità.
>
> *My assistant has been very **diligent** in getting the things entrusted to him done at work: he has shown a lot of professionalism.*

subdolo
sly, sneaky

Subdolo means *sly* or *sneaky*.

> Ilenia ha dimostrato di essere una persona **subdola**, tradendo la fiducia dei suoi amici per una misera somma di denaro.
>
> *Ilenia has proven to be a **sneaky** person, betraying the trust of her friends for a paltry amount of money.*

stantio
stale
old-fashioned

Stantio (*pl.* **stantii, stantie**) can mean *stale* when we talk about bread. It can also be figuratively used to refer to ideas that have passed their sell-by date! In Italy, there is nothing worse than sitting down at a restaurant and being given some stale bread to munch on before dinner:

> Oggi al ristorante mi hanno servito del pane **stantio**, duro come la pietra.
>
> *Today at the restaurant they served me **stale** bread, hard as a rock.*

tale
such

Tale (or **tali** in the plural) is a demonstrative adjective that is variable only in number. It means *such* or *such (a)*. The indefinite article (**un, una**, *etc.*) often precedes it:

> Questa pasta è **una tale schifezza** che ho dovuto lasciarla dopo il primo boccone.
>
> *This pasta is **such crap** that I had to leave it after the first bite.*

Tale/tali can also be used to substitute for **questo** or **quello** but *only when* the person or thing that it references has been previously indicated in your phrase:

> Eccoci arrivati alla celebre Villa del Casale di Piazza Armerina: **tale** dimora fu costruita all'incirca intorno alla prima metà del IV secolo d.C.
>
> *Here we have arrived at the famous Villa del Casale of Piazza Armerina: **this** dwelling was constructed roughly around the first half of the fourth century AD.*

In order to communicate precisely and correctly in Italian, it is important to determine the position of the adjective with respect to the noun that it modifies because its position relative to the noun can alter the adjectives meaning. To best understand this, let us look at an example of an Italian commercial from the 1980's (you can watch the commercial here: https://www.youtube.com/watch?v=xOSWSI5iLR8). In the commercial the workman says:

"Per dipingere una parete grande, ci vuole **un pennello grande**."

"To paint a large wall, it requires a large brush."

The policeman responds:

"Non ci vuole **un pennello grande**, ma **un grande pennello**!"

It doesn't take a large brush, but a high quality brush!"

Altering the placement of the adjective changes the meaning of the adjective, **grande**. **Un pennello grande** means *a large brush* (its dimensions) whereas **un grande pennello** means *a high quality brush*. From the example, we can deduce that if the adjective is placed **before the noun** its meaning and expressiveness is somewhat muted; if the adjective **comes after the noun**, it acquires a greater significance.

When there are several adjectives that accompany a noun, Italian calls for adjectives with a **subjective quality** (a personal judgment or evaluation) to come first and those more **objective** in nature (something real or measurable) to come after:

Il vaso che ho comprato è un **bellissimo** ed **elegante** (*subjective*) esemplare **cinese** (*objective*).

*The vase that I bought is a **beautiful** and **elegant Chinese** copy.*

When adjectives are modifying nouns directly (and not as predicates, as seen in the previous example), placing the adjective **before the noun** gives it a **subjective** meaning whereas placing it **after the noun** gives the adjective an **objective** one:

Hai assaggiato quella **deliziosa** e **succulenta** (*subjective*) torta?

Did you taste that delicious and succulent cake?

In the example above, a cake that I think tastes *delicious* and *succulent* might not receive the same esteem from someone else.

Ho prestato a Marco una calcolatrice **scientifica** (*objective*).

I loaned Marco a scientific calculator.

The quality of the calculator -- *scientific* -- is *objective*: it is something that is real that we can measure based on the functions that it can perform.

Giovanni è un uomo **povero**: ha perso il lavoro e la casa. (*objective*)

Giovanni is a poor man: he lost his job and home.

In the example above, the usage is *objective* because we can measure Giovanni's net worth by looking at his bills and bank statements. It is a quality that is real and measurable.

Giovanni è un **povero** uomo: è stato lasciato dalla sua ragazza.(*subjective*)

Giovanni is a poor man: he was dumped by his girlfriend.

In the example above, he is *poor* not in the financial sense, but in a figurative one. *Poor* in this case means *unhappy* or *miserable*. However, it is subjective because while you might see him as *poor* because his girlfriend dumped him, another friend might consider it a blessing in disguise since she was never very nice to begin with!

5 Pronouns
Pronomi

Pronouns substitute for nouns. In English, pronouns substitute only other nouns: *The cat is meowing. It is sitting in the window.* In our example, the pronoun, *it*, replaces the noun, *cat*. In Italian, pronouns function the same way, except that Italian pronouns can also act as substitutes for adjectives, verbs, and even whole phrases.

This chapter will look at the following types of pronouns:

1. subject pronouns (**pronomi personali soggetto**)

2. direct & indirect object pronouns (**pronomi personali complemento**)

3. reflexive pronouns (**pronomi riflessivi**)

4. possessive pronouns (**pronomi possessivi**)

5. demonstrative pronouns (**pronomi dimostrativi**)

6. relative pronouns (**pronomi relativi**)

7. indefinite pronouns (**pronomi indefiniti**)

8. interrogative and exclamative pronouns (**pronomi interrogativi** e **esclamativi**)

Subject pronouns
Pronomi personali soggetto

Subject pronouns (**pronomi personali soggetto**) were highlighted in Chapter 1:

singular	plural
io (*I*)	noi (*we*)
tu (*you*)	voi (*you*)
lui (*he*)/lei (*she*) Lei (*you, formal*)	loro (*they*)

In Italian, subject pronouns can be omitted since the verb endings (**le desinenze**) indicate the number of the verb. Subject pronouns, though, should be employed when:

- the verb ending is ambiguous, such as with the present subjunctive (**congiuntivo presente**) where the singular forms of the verb are identical:

All'università i miei colleghi sono convinti che **io** sia un somaro.

*At university my colleagues are convinced that **I** am a dunce.*

- the subject pronoun should be used when using indefinite moods when the subject of the dependent phrase is different from the independent one:

Non avendo **lei** mai praticato alcuno sport, l'istruttore ritenne necessario dedicarle un programma di allenamento personalizzato.

*Since **she** never had done any sport, the instructor thought it was necessary to dedicate a personalized training program to her.*

• the subject or subjects need to be highlighted or contrasted:

Potete supplicarci quanto volete, ma **noi** in quel locale non ci metteremo piede! **Voi** fate pure quel che vi pare!

*You can beg us as much as you want, but **we** will not set foot in that place! But **you** do what you want!*

• the verb is not stated:

"Ragazzi, chi vuole partecipare al viaggio di istruzione di fine anno?"

"Guys, who wants to take part in the field trip at the end of the year?"

"**Noi** tutti, professoressa!"

*"**We** do*, Professor!"*

*Note the final line (**We** *do, Professor!*). The use of the subject pronoun on its own is the equivalent of *subject pronoun* + *do/does/did* in English.

Direct & indirect object pronouns
Pronomi personali complemento

Before we begin this section, a quick **ripasso** of some grammar is in order. In English, the *direct object* receives the action of the verb. In Italian, the *direct object* is known as the **complemento oggetto**. It is never preceded by a preposition and, just like English, asks the question *who* or *what* and receives the action of the verb:

> Marco lancia **la palla.**
>
> *Marco is throwing **the ball.***

In the example above, **la palla** (*the ball*) is the receiver of the action: it is the **complemento oggetto** (our *direct object*). If we want to substitute the noun with a pronoun, we must use a **pronome diretto** (also known as a **pronome personale complemento oggetto**):

singular		plural	
mi	*me*	ci	*us*
ti	*you*	vi	*you*
lo	*him*	li	*their (m.)*
la	*her*	le	*their (f.)*

Da notare:
The pronouns profiled on this page are known as **pronomi in forma atona** (*atonal*).

They are called this because they do not have their own accent and *lean on* the verb, coming before the verb or attaching to the imperative or

The pronoun **La** is the formal *you* pronoun. It is always capitalized. *Remember* that **lo/la/li/le** are selected based on the gender and number of the item for which they substitute. The formal pronoun **La** is used for both men and women.

Now, let's turn back to Marco and the ball. Let us replace the direct object **la palla** with the correct pronoun:

> Marco **la** lancia.
>
> *Marco is throwing **it**.*

Now let us say that Marco threw the ball to his friend, Gianna:

> Marco lancia la palla **a Gianna**.
>
> Marco is throwing **Gianna** the ball.
>
> or
>
> *Marco throws the ball **to Gianna**.*

In Italian, the indirect object, when it is a noun or proper noun, is always formed with the preposition **a** (+ **noun/ proper noun**, as seen in our example above). This Italian grammatical construction is known as **il complemento di termine** and expresses where the action ends in the phrase (just like the indirect object in English). In other words, Marco throws the ball (action), which sails through the air (receiving the action) and ends up with Gianna (where the action ends, **il termine**). The indirect object also asks the questions *to whom* or *for whom*.

I complementi di termine are just one of the many **complementi indiretti** in Italian. These **complimenti indiretti** complete the meaning of the verb or some other element in the phrase (such as the subject or another prepositional phrase), often involving prepositions (but not always). For example, many time expressions, such as **due ore** or **il 2 settembre** are **complementi indiretti**.

122

In Italian, there are many kinds of **complementi indiretti** (the chapter on prepositions addresses this in the section on **analisi logica**).

Below are the indirect object pronouns (**pronomi personali complemento indiretto**):

singular		plural	
mi	*me*	ci	*us*
ti	*you*	vi	*you*
gli	*(to/for) him*	gli*	*their (m.)*
le	*(to/for) her*	gli*	*their (f.)*

*gli is used for the *m. sing.* and *m.* and *f. plur.*

If we want to substitute our indirect object **Gianna** for a pronoun, we would write:

> Marco **le*** lancia la palla.
>
> *Marco is throwing her the ball.*
>
> or
>
> *Marco is throwing the ball to her.*

*(le = a Gianna)

Now if we want to replace both objects with pronouns (**il complemento oggetto** and **il complemento di termine**), we would write:

> Marco **gliela** lancia.
>
> *Marco is throwing it to her.*

The chart below shows how object pronouns in Italian are combined (note that the italicized pronouns are indirect object pronouns; the bold ones are direct object pronouns):

	lo	**la**	**li**	**le**	**ne**
mi	me lo	me la	me li	me le	me ne
ti	te lo	te la	te li	te le	te ne
*gli/le**	glielo	gliela	glieli	gliele	gliene
*si**	se lo	se la	se li	se le	se ne
ci	ce lo	ce la	ce li	ce le	ce ne
vi	ve lo	ve la	ve li	ve le	ve ne

same forms for both third-person singular and plural

A difficulty many students face as they study Italian is that indirect objects (**complementi di termine**) can exist without a direct object. In English, there must be a direct object for there to be an indirect object. Students should be aware there are many verbs in Italian that do not require direct objects and take only indirect objects. **Piacere** is one example. Other verbs that fall into this category are: **dare, dire, domandare, insegnare, mandare, mostrare, offrire, portare, preparare, regalare, rendere, riportare, scrivere, telefonare**, etc.

For example: Take the verb **telefonare**. In English, it is a **transitive verb**: *I phoned him.* In English, *him* is the direct object because it receives the action of the verb. In Italian, **telefonare** is intransitive and cannot have a direct object. Therefore, *I phoned him* = **Gli ho telefonato** (I Io telefonato **a lui**). In Italian, it requires **complemento di termine**.

In English, *indirect objects* can also answer the question *for whom,* which is expressed with a different kind of **complemento** in Italian: **il complemento di vantaggio.** This **complemento** asks the question **per chi** (*for whom*). Remember that the English equivalent to the *indirect object* in Italian is a **complemento indiretto** that can be either a **complemento di termine** -- with the preposition, **a +** **nome** or indirect object pronoun. They can also be **complementi di vantaggio** (with the preposition, **per +** **nome**), which asks the question **per chi** / *for whom.* Note that indirect object pronouns can also replace **complementi di vantaggio,** as seen below:

Marco compra una giacca **per Gianna.**

Marco is buying a jacket for Gianna.

Marco **le*** compra una giacca.

Marco is buying her a jacket.
Marco is buying a jacket for her.

*le = per Gianna

It should be pointed out that **il complemento di termine** in Italian does not always depend on the verb. Many adjectives take **complementi di termine,** such as **utile, inutile, simile, dissimile, identico, uguale, contrario, caro, ostile, avverso, vicino, prossimo, adatto, necessario, propenso, incline, attento,** to name a few.

For example, the adjective, **adatto:**

Questo gioco non è **adatto ai bambini**.

This game is not suitable for children.

In the phrase above, **ai bambini** is **il complemento di termine**: it would not be an indirect object in English!

Below are some further examples showing the use of direct and indirect object pronouns in Italian:

complemento oggetto (*direct object*)

Mamma ha fatto **una torta** buonissima: **la** porterò stasera ai miei amici!

Mom made a wonderful cake: I will bring it to my friends tonight!

complemento indiretto (*indirect object*)

Ad un caffè in Piazza San Marco un performer **ci*** ha cantato un'aria da "I due foscari".

At a café in the Piazza San Marco, a performer sang us an aria from I due foscari.

*ci = *a noi*

complemento oggetto & complemento indiretto
(direct and indirect object pronouns together)

"Mauro, puoi dire a tua sorella di chiamarmi, quando la vedrai?"

"Mauro, can you tell your sister to call me when you see her?"

"Certo, **glielo** dirò!"

"Of course, I will tell her (to)."

In the example above, the pronoun, **lo** (in **glielo**), refers to the act of calling the speaker (**lo** = **di chiamarmi**). This use of the pronoun **lo** to replace a phrase or part of one is common in Italian.

Tonic pronouns
Forme toniche dei pronomi

Tonic or *stressed* pronouns (**le forme forti o toniche**) can be used both with prepositions and without. The tonic pronouns are:

singular	plural
me	noi
te	voi
lui (*m.*) lei (*f.*)	loro

Tonic pronouns can be used:

1. as direct objects (**complementi oggetti**), coming after the verb. It can immediately follow the verb or appear somewhat later in the phrase, as well

> **Scegli** ancora una volta **me**!
>
> *Choose me once again!*

Note that at times they can also become *before* the verb. In spoken Italian, their pronunciation must be *accented*. This construction emphasizes the direct object that receives the action:

> **Lei**, ti ho detto di chiamare, non **me**!
>
> *I told you to call HER, not ME!*

2. as indirect objects or **complementi di termine** (**a + pronome tonico**)

128

> **A te** darò questo compito.
>
> (**Ti** darò questo compito)
>
> *I will give this assignment **to you**.*

Attenzione: Indirect object pronouns have the same meaning as their tonic counterparts *only when the tonic pronouns are used with the preposition* **a** (**mi** = **a me, ti** = **a te, gli** = **a lui, le** = **a lei, ci** = **a noi, vi** = **a voi, gli** = **a loro**) _and_ answer the question *to what/to whom* or with the preposition, **per**, when they answer the question *for whom* (**per chi**).

3. with other prepositions (such as **da, per, presso, secondo,** etc.) to form other kinds of prepositional phrases (**complementi indiretti**). These **complementi** can come both *before* or *after* the verb:

> Un tipo losco si è appena seduto **accanto a me**.
>
> **Accanto a me** si è appena seduto un tipo losco.
>
> *A shady guy just sat **next to me**.*

When tonic pronouns follow the verb (without a preposition), they often add emphasis and are often used in pairs to dispel ambiguity or to emphasize exclusivity. For example, imagine that you are a witness to an argument between your friend, Gianna, and her boyfriend, Antonino. She is upset because she is afraid he might be cheating on her with his ex-girlfriend. He responds:

> Amore, non ti ho mai tradito! Amo **te**, non **lei**!
>
> *My love, I have never cheated on you! I love you, not her!*

In the example above, the use of the tonic pronoun emphasizes that he loves *her* and no one else.

Tonic pronouns are also used after **come** and **quanto (non sono bravo come te)** and in exclamations (**beato te, povero me**). They can also be reinforced with the word **stesso** (which agrees in gender and number with the noun it modifies: Daniela pensa sempre a **se stessa!**). The tonic form **te** is also used when **tu** follows the subject pronoun **io** (**io e te** = *you and I*). When the second person singular comes before **io**, the subject pronoun is used, *not* the tonic pronoun: **tu e io** (*you and I*).

Lastly, **loro**, can also be used in place of **gli**. The tonic pronoun **loro** comes after the verb, but **gli** comes before the verb. **Gli** should be avoided *if* its use would create unecessary ambiguity. **Gli** is often preferred in spoken Italian:

> Il capo **gli** ha ingiustamente affidato l'incarico di controllare le fasi del progetto.
> *or*
> Il capo ha ingiustamente affidato **(a) loro** l'incarico di controllare le fasi del progetto.
>
> *The boss wrongly trusted **them** with the task of checking the phases of the project.*

Reflexive pronouns
Pronomi riflessivi

Reflexive pronouns (**pronomi riflessivi**) refer back to the subject, translating as *myself, yourself, him/herself,* etc.

singular	plural
mi	ci
ti	vi
si	si

Reflexive pronouns are used with many verbs. We learned about a couple of them in Chapter 1, such as **alzarsi** and **svegliarsi**.

Some further examples of reflexive pronouns can be seen below:

Vi mobilitaste per una giusta causa, e per questo mi sento in dovere di rispettarvi.

You rallied for a just cause, and, for this reason, I feel duty bound to respect you.

Serena e Paolo **sacrificarono se stessi** per il gruppo: li stimo davvero tanto!

*Serena and Paolo **are sacrificing themselves** for the group: I really think highly of them!*

Reflexives can also be formed using the tonic pronoun **sé**. Remember, though, that the accent is dropped when it is paired with **stesso** or **medesimo**.

Da notare:
Remember that the reflexive pronoun is a part of the verb: its presence is obligatory.

Omitting it has the potential to change the meaning of your phrases:

È proprio della sua indole **farsi del male**.

It's in his nature to hurt himself.

È proprio della sua indole **fare del male**.

It is in his nature to harm (others).

Apart from being used reflexively (**me stesso/a, noi stessi/e**), reflexive pronouns can also be used when the action is reciprocal, as in the English *each other*:

> È una vita che non vedo Maura. Quando **ci siamo visti** alla stazione **ci siamo baciati** con passione!
>
> *It's been ages since I saw Maura. When **we saw each other**, we **kissed each other** passionately!*

Reflexives can also be used when we want to emphasize an action or emphasize some emotional aspect of an action that the subject is performing:

> **Mi sto mangiando** tutta la torta: non riesco a smettere!
>
> *I am eating all of the cake: I can't stop!*
>
> **Se l'è bevuta** tutta la bottiglia di vino?
>
> *You drank the whole bottle of wine?*

132

Possessive pronouns
Pronomi possessivi

Possessive pronouns (**pronomi possessivi**) are used to indicate possession. In Italian, the possessive pronouns are:

singular		plural	
m.	*f.*	*m.*	*f.*
il mio	la mia	i miei	le mie
il tuo	la tua	i tuoi	le tue
il suo	la sua	i suoi	le sue
il nostro	la nostra	i nostri	le nostre
il vostro	la vostra	i vostri	le vostre
il loro	la loro	i loro	le loro

The article is always used with possessive pronouns. The invariable pronoun, **altrui,** is also possessive and translate as *other people* or *other's,* whereas **proprio,** translates to *one's own* (see the chapter on adjectives for rules on using **proprio**).

Here are some examples that illustrate the usage of possessive pronouns in Italian:

> Quando si parla di errori commessi, siamo sempre pronti a criticare **gli altrui**, ma mai i propri!
>
> *When we speak of errors made, we are always ready to criticize **other people's** (mistakes) but never our own.*

Io e mio fratello abbiamo comprato per ciascuno un nuovo pc, ma **il mio** è decisamente più performante **del suo!**"

*My brother and I each bought ourselves a new computer, but **mine** is decidedly more high-performance than **his**!*

Tra i vari progetti, **il vostro** è senza dubbio il migliore.

*Among the various projects, **yours** is without a doubt the best.*

Benvenuti nel mio residence! **Questa** è **casa mia**, mentre **quello** laggiù è **l'accesso** per raggiungere il mare e la piscina.

*Welcome to my home! **This** is **my home**, while that down **there** is **the gate** to get to the beach and the pool.*

Demonstrative pronouns
Pronomi dimostrativi

Demonstrative pronouns (**pronomi dimostrativi**) in Italian correspond to the English, *this* or *that*. In Italian, the three most common demonstrative pronouns are: **questo** (*this*), **quello** (*that*), and **codesto** (*this*). Their forms can be seen below:

singular		plural	
m.	f.	m.	f.
questo	questa	questi	queste
codesto	codesta	codesti	codeste
quello	quella	quelli	quelle

Remember that these pronouns are variable and agree in gender and number with the noun that they refer to!

There are other demonstrative pronouns in Italian. The pronoun, **costoro** (also **costui** and **costei**) means *those people*, and it is often used in a derogatory manner:

Chi sono **costoro**? Chi si credono di essere per entrare nella mia proprietà?!

*Who are **those people**? Who do they think they are coming onto my property?!*

Colui and **colei che** are used to refer to people who are some distance away from the person speaking and the person listening. They translate to *that man/woman or that person*:

> **Colui** o **colei** che ha combinato questo scempio, per
> favore, abbia il coraggio di farsi avanti!
>
> *That man or woman who caused the wreck, please, have
> the courage to step forward!*

Ciò can also be used as a demonstrative pronoun either as
the subject or as a complement. It translate as *this* or *that*:

> Perché oggi non lavorano? Tutto **ciò** [questo] è
> davvero inaccettabile!
>
> *Why are they not working today? All of **this** is really
> unacceptable!*

The pronoun **lo** can also act as a demonstrative pronoun
meaning **questa cosa**. In English, we might say *it*, as in the
example below:

> "**L'** ho detto più volte: la città ha bisogno di puntare
> sull'arte."
>
> *"I said **it** many times: the city needs to look to art."*

The particle, **ne**, can also mean **di questa cosa**. It can
replace partitive constructions. In English, it would
translate as *of it:*

> "La pasta era davvero deliziosa, ma non **ne** [di questa
> cosa] voglio più, grazie!
>
> *The pasta was really delicious, but I don't want any more **of
> it**, thank you!"*

The particle **ci** can also be used demonstratively, meaning *of it*, *on it*, etc.:

> "Verrai alla mia laurea?"
>
> *"Will you come to my graduation?"*
>
> "Certo, **ci** puoi scommettere!"
>
> *"Of course, you can count on it!"*

Relative pronouns
Pronomi relativi

Relative pronouns (**pronomi relativi**) are one of the most difficult aspects of Italian grammar. In English, relative pronouns refer to *antecedents*, nouns in the independent clause (**la proposizione reggente** or *the 'ruling' clause*) that "anchor" the two phrases. The relative pronoun stands in for the antecedent in the dependent clause.

In Italian, relative pronouns function the same way, although, not all relative pronouns in Italian require antecedents.

che
that, who

The most common relative pronoun is **che**, which can mean *who* or *that*. It can be the subject or the direct object (**il soggetto o il complemento oggetto**) of the dependent clause (**la proposizione subordinata**). It is important to note that **che** is invariable: it does not change form to match the gender or number of the antecedent.

Avviso!
While relative pronouns can often be omitted in English, they are *always* required in Italian!

Che is equivalent to **il/la quale/i quali/le quali** but *only when the latter are the subject of the dependent clause.*

La ragazza **che** hai conosciuto ieri sera è mia sorella: guarda un po' che coincidenza!

*The girl **who** you met yesterday evening is my sister: looks a bit like a coincidence!*

il quale
that, who, whom

Il/la quale and **i quali/le quali** are variable relative pronouns that serve either as subjects of dependent clauses or as **complementi indiretti** with prepositions. This form is preferred to avoid confusion regarding the antecedent.

It is extremely *rare* for this form to be used as a direct object but occurs often in formal writing. In the example above, **il/la quale** would not be correct.

Remember: this form is *variable* and agrees in gender and number with the antecedent:

> Non conosci Roberta? È **la** ragazza **alla quale** ho dato lezioni private di pianoforte.
>
> *Do you know Roberta? She is the girl **to whom** I gave private piano lessons.*

cui
that, which, whom, who

Cui is an invariable relative pronoun that can mean *that, which, whom,* and even *where.* Its translation depends on its function in the phrase. **Cui** has two roles:

- as the **complemento indiretto** of a phrase and is always used with a preposition:

> L'uomo **(a) cui** hai prestato soccorso è un ricco signore: saprà come ricompensarti."
>
> *The man, **who** you helped, is a rich gentleman: he will know how to reward you.*

or

- with the definite article (**il, la, i, le**), it corresponds to the possessive relative pronoun, *whose*

Here are some further examples using **cui**:

Hai presente quel tipo, **di cui** non ricordo il nome? Mi ha chiesto un appuntamento!

*Do you remember that guy **whose** name I don't remember? He asked me for a date!*

Da notare!
Note that the preposition, **a**, with **cui** can be omitted *only* when it functions as the indirect object (**complemento di termine**). In this phrase, **a** would be required because **a cui** functions as a **complemento di moto a luogo:**

La mostra d'arte contemporanea **a cui** sono andata ieri sera è stata davvero interessante!

*The contemporary art show **that** I went **to** yesterday evening was really interesting!*

La cava **da cui** ricavano il materiale edile per il nuovo complesso è a rischio di crollo!

*The quarry **where** they were extracting building material for the new complex is at risk of collapsing!*

Il motivo **per cui** non mi rivolgo a te è perché sei del tutto inaffidabile!

*The reason (**that**) I am not speaking you is because you are completely untrustworthy!*

La città **in cui** ho soggiornato la settimana scorsa è al confine tra la Germania e l'Austria.

*The city **where** I stayed last week is on the border between Germany and Austria.*

I progetti proposti, **tra cui** vi era anche il mio, erano tutti molto interessanti.

*The proposed projects, **among which** there was also mine, were all very interesting.*

> Il numero di telefono **con cui** ti ho contattato è
> quello dell'ufficio, non di casa.
>
> *The telephone number (**that**) I contacted you **on** is the office
> one, not the home.*

These examples below employ **cui** as the possessive relative
pronoun, whose:

> L'aloe vera, **delle cui** [di + le + cui] proprietà
> benefiche [delle proprietà benefiche della quale] sono
> venuto a conoscenza da poco, è una pianta che
> predilige i climi caldi e secchi.
>
> *Aloe vera, **whose** beneficial properties I learned about only
> recently, is a plant that prefers warm and dry climates.*

> Sonia, **la cui** sfacciataggine [della quale la
> sfacciataggine] è nota in tutto l'ambiente
> universitario, ha fatto un esame davvero
> imbarazzante.
>
> *Sonia, **whose** impudence is noted all over academia, had a
> really embarrassing exam.*

chi
who

Chi is invariable and refers only to people and serves only
as the subject of the phrase in the singular. Students of
Italian should not confuse the English relative pronoun
who with **chi** except for the instance just noted. It can be
translated as he who/she who/people who/the person who.

The relative pronouns **che, cui**, and **il quale** should be
used instead to refer to the English relative pronoun, who.

You can see an example of its usage below:

> **Chi** [colui il quale] dice che gli animali non soffrono, non merita alcuna considerazione!
>
> *People who say that animals don't suffer do not deserve any consideration!*

Indefinite pronouns
Pronomi indefiniti

Indefinite pronouns (**pronomi indefiniti**) refer to one or more unspecified people, objects or places. The following indefinite pronouns come up often in Italian and are worth learning: **qualcosa, chiunque, ognuno, niente, nulla,** and **nessuno**.

While some indefinite pronouns can also be used as adjectives, these profiled here are strictly pronouns.

qualcosa
something

The pronoun **qualcosa** means *something*. While it ends in **-a**, it is masculine.

> Paola mi ha sussurrato **qualcosa**, mentre eravamo a lezione, ma non ho capito un tubo!"
>
> *Paola mumbled **something** to me while we were in class, but I didn't understand a thing.*

chiunque
anybody, anyone

Chiunque means *anyone* or *anybody* when used as an indefinite pronoun. It can also be used as a relative pronoun to mean *whoever* or *anyone/anybody who* (note the use of the subjunctive in our example below):

> **Chiunque** sia stato a distruggere questo monumento, la pagherà cara.
>
> ***Whoever** was destroying this monument will pay dearly!*

143

ognuno
everyone, everbody
each

Ognuno means *everyone* or *everybody,* but it can also mean *each* when used with a preposition and a tonic pronoun:

> Ad **ognuno di noi** verrà donata una targa per ricordare questo grande evento.
>
> *A plaque to remember this great event will be donated to each of us.*

niente & nulla
nothing, none

Niente means *nothing* or *anything.* In English, double negatives are to be avoided (*I do not want anything*), whereas in Italian, they are common (**Non voglio niente**):

> Ho già detto a voi giornalisti che non ho **niente** da dichiarare!
>
> *I already told you journalists that I have **nothing** to say!*

Nulla means nothing in Italian, and it is a synonym for **niente**:

> A **nulla** è servito fare la ramanzina a Stefano: ha bevuto come una spugna e adesso sta vomitando l'anima!
>
> *It didn't do any good scolding Stefano: he drank like a fish, and he is now spewing his guts out.*

144

> *Da notare!* Like nulla and niente, the pronoun,
> **qualcosa**, can be used with the prepositions, **di** and
> **da**:
>
> qualcosa **da** + **infinito**:
>
> Hai **qualcosa da aggiungere** alla discussione?
> *Do you have something to add to the discussion?*
>
> qualcosa **di** + **aggettivo**:
>
> Oggi ho proprio voglia di **qualcosa di buono**!
> *Today I am really in the mood for something good!*

Before infinitives, **nulla** and **niente** are followed by the
preposition **da**. Before adjectives, they are followed by the
preposition **di**:

niente/nulla da + **infinito**:

> Non ho nulla **da regalarti**.
>
> *I have nothing to give to you for a gift.*

niente/nulla di + **aggettivo**:

> Non c'è niente **di rassicurante** in quel che è appena
> accaduto.
>
> *There is nothing reassuring in what just happened.*

nessuno

no one, nobody
anyone, anybody

Nessuno means no one or nobody in negative phrases. In English, since we avoid double negatives, it can also translate as anyone or anybody. In Italian, double negatives are common:

> Da quando sono stata lasciata, non ho mai chiesto a **nessuno** di essere confortata.
>
> *Since I had been dumped, I never asked to be comforted by anyone.*

Niente, **nessuno,** and **nulla** (when they are placed before the verb) do not require another negation:

incorrect: **nessuno non** mi vuole.
correct: **nessuno** mi vuole.

If either of these three pronouns follow the verb, the negation is necessary (**Non** è **nulla** di grave = *It isn't anything bad*).

Interrogative & exclamative pronouns
Pronomi interrogativi e esclamativi

Interrogative pronouns (**pronomi interrogativi**) are used to formulate questions (**domande**). In English, our *question words* are *what, which, whose* (**di chi**) and *who?* In Italian, the pronouns are **che, chi, quale,** and **quanto**.

In Italian, interrogative pronouns can also be used as exclamations, which are used to express *joy, fear,* or *surprise.*

che
what

Che is invariable and translates as *what*. **Cosa** and **Che cosa** are informal substitutes for **che** when asking *what?*

interrogative:

> **Che** ho fatto di male per meritarmi tutta questa cattiveria da parte tua?
>
> *What did I do wrong to deserve all this meanness from you?*

exclamative:

> **Che** meraviglioso regalo mi hai fatto!
>
> *What a marvelous gift you have given me!*

chi
who, whom

Chi is invariable and is used with people. It translates to *who* or *whom*.

interrogative:

> **Chi** vuole venire con me stasera al cinema?
>
> *Who wants to come with me to the movies tonight?*

exclamation:

> **Chi** l'avrebbe mai detto che ti saresti fatta suora!
>
> *Who would have ever said that you would have become a nun!*

Di chi is used to enquire about ownership and is equivalent to the English *whose + noun:*

> **Di chi** è quella giacca lì?
>
> *Whose jacket is that there?*
>
> È **di Marco**. L'ha dimenticata per l'ennesima volta!
>
> *It's Marco's. He forgot it for the umpteenth time!*

quale
what, which

Quale means *which* or *what*. Before the third person singular of **essere**, the pronoun is truncated, *not* elided (**Qual è** *but never* **Qual'è!**). It is variable, either singular (**quale**) or plural (**quali**), depending on the noun it refers to. Its gender remains invariable.

interrogative:

> **Quali** dolci vuoi che prepari per la cena di domani sera?
>
> *Which desserts do you want me to prepare for tomorrow evening's dinner?*

exclamation:

> Ciao Andrea! **Quale** onore averti qui fra noi!
>
> *Ciao, Andrea! What an honor to have you here among us!*

quanto
how much (sing.)
how many (pl.)

Quanto is variable, agreeing in gender and number with the noun to which it refers. It translates as *how much* in the singular and *how many* in the plural.

interrogative:

> **Quanto** vuole per questo splendido piatto in porcellana?
>
> *How much does he want for this splendid porcelain plate?*

exclamation:

> **Quanto** vorrei averti qui con me stasera...
>
> *I would very much like to have you here with me tonight...*

Da notare!   **Pronoun Placement**

Atonal pronouns generally precede the verb, but there are situations where it can come after or attach to infinitives and other indefinite forms. Let's examine those situations:

- Atonal pronouns attach to the **tu** and **voi** forms of the imperative in affirmative and negative phrases (but can come before negative informal commands *but must come before* formal affirmative and negative commands):

    Michele, porta**mi** il metro! Voglio misurare la porta.
    Michele, bring me the ruler! I want to measure the door.

    Ragazzi, aiutate**mi** a spostare le scatole!
    Guys, help me move the boxes!

    Non **mi sgridare** così! Non sono tuo figlio!
    Non **sgridarmi** così! Non sono tuo figlio!
    Don't scold me like that! I am not your son!

    Scusi, signore, **mi può dire** come si arriva alla stazione? Sono disperato!
    Excuse me, sir, please can you tell me how to get to the station? I am desperate!

- Atonal pronouns can also attach to infinitives:

    Vado a aiutar**la**, torno dopo!
    I am going to help her, I'll back back after!

- With modal verbs, atonal pronouns can attach to the infinitive that follows or come before the modal:

    Devo dir**ti** una cosa importante!
    Ti devo dire una cosa importante!

    I have something important to tell you.

continued...

- Atonal pronouns can also attach to past participles and gerund forms:

Una volta dato**gli** confidenza, quel ragazzo non ti lascerà più in pace!
Once you opened the door to him, that guy will never leave you alone!

Avendo**ti** già detto come stanno le cose, non ho più alcun motivo di vederti.
Having told you how things are going, I don't have a reason to see you anymore.

- Atonal pronouns double the starting consonant of the pronoun when the imperative is *truncated* with verbs, such as **andare**, **dare**, **dire**, **fare**, and **stare**:

Da**mmi** una mano!
Give me a hand!

Di**cci** dove dobbiamo andare!
Tell us where we have to go!

Va**ttene**, mi rompi le scatole!
Get out of here, you are bothering me!

Sta**ttene** a letto, hai la febbre alta!
Stay in bed, you have a high fever!

Fa**mmi** vedere quello che hai rotto!
Let me see what you broke!

Take note that the pronoun, **gli**, does not double its initial consonant:

Da**gli** una mano, non riesce a seguire le istruzioni.
Give him a hand, he can't follow instructions.

continued...

• Atonal pronouns also attach to the adverb, **ecco**:

Marco: "Maria, dove sono i tuoi genitori?"
Genitori: "**Eccoci** qua! Finalmente siamo arrivati!"

Marco: "Maria, where are your parents?"
Parents: "Here we are! We finally arrived!"

Da notare!   Pronouns & Past Participles

Pronouns can change how past participles behave in compound tenses. Let's go over some rules below that govern the use of pronouns and past participles:

1. When the auxiliary is **avere**, the past participle agrees in gender and number with the direct object pronouns: **lo, la, le** and **li**.

2. Only pronouns, **lo** and **la** elide with the conjugated forms of avere (**l'ho comprata ieri!**)

3. Agreement between the other direct object pronouns, **mi, ti, ci** and **vi**, and the past participle is optional.

4. Indirect object pronouns *never* influence the gender and number of the past participle. When object pronouns are combined, the *direct object pronoun* or **ne** determines the agreement.

5. In compound tenses where the auxiliary is **essere**, the past participle agrees in gender and number with the subject. The only exception is with some reflexives verbs. If one of the direct object pronouns is present, the past participle *will agree* in gender and number with the direct object pronoun.

6. In the presence of the pronoun, **ne**, the past participle agrees in gender and number with the noun replaced by **ne**.

6 Adverbs
Avverbi

Adverbs are words that modify a verb, adjective or another adverb. They are *invariable* (**invariabili**): they do not alter themselves to reflect the gender or number of the word that they modify. In English, we commonly recognize them because they end in **-ly** while in Italian with the suffix, -**mente**. However, not all adverbs end in **-ly** (or -**mente**).

In Italian there are seven categories of adverbs:

1. adverbs of place (**luogo**)

2. adverbs of time (**tempo**)

3. qualifiers (**qualificativi**)

4. quantity (**quantità**)

5. negations, affirmations and judgments (**negazioni, affermazioni, giudizio**)

6. interrogatives and exclamations (**interrogativi e esclamazioni**)

7. words like **ecco** (**presentativi**)

155

Formation of adverbs

Formazioni degli avverbi

Adverbs generally come before the words that they modify, although the placement can be affected by a number of factors.

In Italian, adverbs come in three types: *simple, derived* and *compound. Simple adverbs* are single words whose only function is to be an adverb. *Derived adverbs* are those that are formed from adjectives or verbs. *Compound adverbs* are those that are made up of two or more words, such as **dappertutto, infatti,** etc. Adverbs can also be phrasal (**locuzioni**), such as **di sera, poco fa**, etc.

To form adverbs from adjectives:

1. Add the suffix -**mente** to the end of the feminine form of the adjective. If the adjective ends in -**e**, simply add -**mente** to the end. Adjectives that end in -**re** or -**le** drop the -**e** and before adding -**mente**:

    largo = > larga = > larga**mente**
    intelligente = > intelligente**mente**
    celere = > celer**mente**
    visibile = > visibil**mente**

2. Adverbs can also be formed by placing the adjective after the expression **in modo**:

    veloce = > **in modo** veloce = velocemente

156

affatto

completely, absolutely
not at all, in the least

This is a useful adverb to know because you will hear it a lot in conversations and while reading. In affirmative phrases, **affatto** means *completely* or *absolutely*. In negative phrases (with **non** or **niente**), it means *not at all* or *in the least*. **Affatto** is often used in a *negative sense* in *affirmative phrases*, especially in spoken Italian. You will hear it being used to mean *not at all* in affirmative phrases, too. In the example below, Marco is explaining to a friend about a recent encounter with their mutual friend, Luigi:

> Ho provato a ragionare con lui, ma abbiamo idee **affatto** compatibili.
>
> *I tried to reason with him, but we have ideas that are **not at all** compatible.*

It is better to use **affatto** in negative constructions, especially in your writing in order to avoid creating ambiguities. Consider the conversation below. A friend of yours wants you make peace with Veronica, who has wronged you:

> "Perché non fate pace, tu e Veronica?"
>
> *"Why don't you and Veronica make peace?"*
>
> "**Niente affatto**! Non sono disposto a perdonarla."
>
> *"**No way!** I am not inclined to forgive her."*

appena
barely, hardly, just

The adverb **appena** is a useful adverb to know and means *just*. It can also mean *barely* or *hardly*. This adverb, when it is part of a compound tense and is not being used as a conjunction (**remember that some words in Italian have more than one function**), comes between the auxiliary and past participle.

Imagine you are out on a date with Claudio, who you just met last week. The date is going well, but you are in a quandary:

> Cosa fare? Claudio mi ha chiesto di andare dopo cena a casa sua, ma ci conosciamo **appena**!
>
> *What to do? Claudio asked me to go to his place after dinner, but we **hardly** know each other!*

domani
tomorrow

The adverb **domani** (like **ieri** and **oggi**) is an important adverb of time and means *tomorrow*. With the preposition **di** preceding the adverb, it translate as *tomorrow's* (**la cena di domani** = *tomorrow's dinner*).

Most adverbs of time tend to come at the beginning of the phrase. Placing them at the end of the phrase can emphasize that something will   most certainly take place *tomorrow* (and not the day after or next week).

Remember: the beginning of the phrase does not necessarily mean it is the first word of the sentence. A sentence made up of two phrases could each have an adverb of time at the beginning of their respective phrases. This can be seen in this example below. Notice that the adverb **domani** is at the beginning of the dependent clause! This rule applies to **ieri** and **oggi**, too.

You are looking to unwind after a long day at work and decide to catch up on the day's events. The news comes on with an important weather alert for tomorrow:

> Al telegiornale hanno detto che **domani** ci sarà un terribile temporale con trombe d'aria: meglio stare attenti!
>
> *On the news they said that **tomorrow** there will be a terrible thunderstorm with tornadoes: better pay attention.*

già
already

Già means *already*. It is an important adverb to know since you will see it and hear it used regularly. These little words in Italian are often missed by students because there are so many of them. Unlike many nouns, their meanings are not obvious. This adverb also goes between the auxiliary and the past participle in compound tenses.

You splurged this week by buying some comic books, and your allowance is now in the hands of the bookstore where you bought them. Your friends want to go out and grab something to eat so you ask your mother for a few extra euro. She responds:

> Sei davvero incredibile! Ti ho dato la paghetta l'altro ieri e vuoi **già** altri soldi?!
>
> *You are really incredible! I gave you the allowance the day before yesterday, and you **already** want more money?*

Nota Bene: Già can also function as an interjection, meaning *"Yes, that's right"* in reply to questions.

ieri
yesterday

Ieri is another important adverb of time that means *yesterday*. Like **domani**, **ieri** can also be used with the preposition **di** to mean *yesterday's* (**di ieri**).

Most adverbs of time tend to come at the beginning of the phrase. Placing them at the end of the phrase can add emphasis, indicating that something definitely took place *yesterday* and not the day before yesterday or even two weeks ago.

In Italy, a lot of jobs, scholarships, and career postings are advertised as competitive entrance exams where candidates compete with one another by taking a test before passing onto subsequent stages of the interview process. It is important to sign up before the deadlines, as our friend, Gianna, unfortunately discovers:

> Accidenti! Ho saputo soltanto ora che **ieri** era l'ultimo giorno utile per iscriversi al concorso!
>
> *Dang! I found out only now that **yesterday** was the last possible day to sign up for the entrance exam!*

laggiù & lassù
down there, down below, over there & up there, up above

The adverbs **laggiù** and **lassù** mean *down there, down below, over there* or *up there, up above*, respectively.

Imagine you have taken some friends to a promontory in your city with the beautiful view in front of you. From there you are able to point out some details that can be seen high above the city:

> Guarda quel piccolo e bianco edificio **laggiù**: era la
> mia scuola elementare, mentre **lassù**, sulla collinetta
> adiacente, si trovano i resti di quel che un tempo era
> l'osservatorio astronomico della cittadella, il suo
> piccolo fiore all'occhiello.
>
> *Look at that small white building **down there**: it was my
> elementary school, while **up there**, on the little hill next to
> it, are the remains of what was once an astronomical
> observatory of the citadel, its small crowning achievement.*

lì & là
there

The adverbs **lì** and **là** mean *there*. While they both mean
there in English, *there is a difference* between the two words in
Italian. **Lì** refers to a place that is not very far from the
speaker; **là** refers to a place that is much farther away.

You are exploring a part of Milan you do not know well.
You realize that you are almost out of cigarettes. There
must be a tobacco shop around here somewhere? You stop
to ask someone on the corner where the nearest tobacco
shop is:

> Tu: "Salve! Potrebbe indicarmi un tabaccheria nelle
> vicinanze?"
>
> *You: "Hi! Could you tell me where the nearest tobacco shop is
> in the neighborhood?*
>
> La persona per strada: "Certo, si trova proprio **lì**,
> accanto alla farmacia."
>
> *The person on the street: "Certainly, it is just **there**, next to
> the pharmacy."*

Now imagine now that you are in Palermo at the port. Your friend, Francesco, comes to meet you and points to the mountain in the distance:

> Il Monte Pellegrino è uno dei promontori più importanti della città di Palermo: è proprio **là** in cima che si trova il santuario di Santa Rosalia, la patrona della città.
>
> *Mount Pellegrino is one of the most important promontories of the city of Palermo: it is just **there** at the top where the Sanctuary of Saint Rosalia, the patron saint of the city, is located.*

mica
by chance; synonym for
non

Mica is an interesting adverb. If you can learn to use it and incorporate it into your speech, you will impress any Italian you meet! **Mica** is a synonym for the adverb **non** and is often used in place of **non**. It can also be used *with* **non,** coming after the verb, to add emphasis to the negation. It also has the meaning *by chance* (**per caso**). When it doesn't come first in the sentence, it follows the verb or, as in compound tenses, comes between the auxiliary and the past participle.

Imagine that you are an Italian teacher and are looking for your class register. Each teacher in Italy is required by law to maintain a register of their students' grades and progress as well as the subjects and material covered. You have misplaced it and ask one of your colleagues nearby if she has seen it:

Hai **mica** visto dove si trova il mio registro di scuola?
Non riesco a trovarlo!

*You haven't by chance seen where my class register is? I
can't find it!*

Mica can also be used as a substitute for **non**:

Carla, perché diavolo hai acceso il mio portatile?
Mica ti ho dato il permesso di usarlo!

*Carla, why the devil did you turn on my laptop? I didn't
give you permission to use it!*

oggi
today

Oggi, like **domani** and **ieri**, is another important adverb
of time that means *today*. Placing the preposition **di** in
front gives it the meaning of *today's* (**la parola di oggi** =
today's word).

Imagine waiting for your first paycheck after starting your
first job:

Dopo tanti mesi di attesa e di lavoro, **oggi** ho
ricevuto il mio primo stipendio: era ora!

*After waiting and working for many months, I finally
received my first paycheck today: finally!*

qui & qua
here

The adverbs **qui** and **qua** both translate as *here*. Like **lì** and **là** mentioned earlier, there is a slight difference between **qui** and **qua**. Both are used with verbs of state and motion (such as **essere** and **andare**), but **qua** has a meaning that indicates a place that is a bit undetermined or generic.

In the example below, the lights have gone out in your apartment. You head down to the ground floor to find the electrical panel, but you are not sure where it might be in the room:

> Non riesco a trovare il quadro elettrico dell'edificio, eppure sono certo che si trova **qua**, da qualche parte!
>
> *I can't find the building's electrical panel, but I am certain it is **here** somewhere!*

Qui, on the other hand, has a meaning that conveys a location that is more 'on target' and precise. In the example below, you have misplaced your backpack. You know it is around here somewhere:

> "Mamma, dove hai messo il mio zaino? Lo cerco da ore!"
>
> *"Mamma, where did you put my backpack? I have been looking for it for hours!"*
>
> "Sei sempre con la testa in aria: è proprio **qui**, davanti a te!"
>
> *"You always have your head in the clouds: it is right **here** in front of you!"*

Milano: Il Duomo (2014)

Da notare!   **Adverb Placement**

Here are some guidelines for the placement of adverbs.

1. Adverbs of time, such as **oggi, domani, ieri**, etc. generally come at the beginning of your phrase:

    Oggi ho un sacco di cose da fare!
    Today, I have a ton of things to do!

    Adverbs can also come at the end of your phrase to highlight the fact that something is happening at *that time* and not any another:

    Ricordati, l'esame di matematica è **domani**! Il professore ha cambiato la data.
    Remember, the math exam is tomorrow! The professor changed the date.

2. The adverb **non** always comes before the verb that it negates:

    Non mi piace quello che hai detto!
    I don't like what you said.

3. Be careful with the adverb, **solo**! Its placement in the phrase can influence what you are trying to say:

    Oggi ho **solo** studiato! (*and did only that*)

    Today, I only studied!

    Oggi ho studiato **solo**! (*and was by myself*)

    Today I studied by myself.

4. In compound tenses, some adverbs come between the auxiliary and the past
    participle, such as **appena, già, solo** (see #3), **mai, nemmeno, proprio**,
    sempre, etc:

    Marco è **appena** uscito di casa: vuoi che gli lasci un messaggio?
    Marco just went out: do you want to leave him a message?

    Non sono **mai** stato a Bologna: è da vedere?
    I have never been to Bologna: is it worth seeing?

5. Adverbs that modify other adjectives or adverbs come before the words that
    they modify:

    Scusi, ho chiesto una bottiglia di acqua **leggermente** frizzante.
    Excuse me, I asked for a bottle of slightly sparkling water.

7 Prepositions
Preposizioni

Prepositions are an invariable part of speech that come before nouns, pronouns, or infinitives. It is important to remember that the selection of the correct preposition depends on the other words that appear in the phrase.

In Italian, there are three types of prepositions:

1. simple (**semplice**) : in Italian, there are nine simple prepositions: **di, a, da, in, con, su, per, tra,** and **fra**.

2. improper (**improprie**): these are words that functions as prepositions but also serve as other parts of speech, such as verbs, adverbs and adjectives: **secondo, vicino, lungo, durante**, etc.

3. phrasal (**locuzioni**): these are phrases made up of two or more words where the final word of the phrase is a preposition, such as: **per mezzo di, a causa di, insieme a,** etc.

Logical analysis
Analisi logica

Prepositions in Italian introduce phrases (**complementi**) that work to enrich the verb or provide additional meaning or specification to the phrase. Each type of prepositional phrase *answers a certain question:* the question asked and the answer to the question forms the basis of *logical analysis* or **analisi logica**.

This aspect of Italian grammar can seem complex for students of Italian, but it is important to understand that prepositional phrases have specific functions in Italian grammar just as they do in English.

Here is a list of some of the most common **complementi** (phrases) in Italian that we will examine in this chapter as we explore the rules of using prepositions. Learning these rules can help in learning to use prepositions correctly.

This list is not exhaustive, but these are some of the more common **complementi** that students will encounter regularly. The following **complementi** are quite common:

1. comparisons (**di paragone**): this phrase answers the question *more/less than someone/something* or *like someone/something*:

   > Gianna è più grande **di Maria**.
   >
   > *Gianna is older **than Maria**.*

2. place (**di stato in luogo**): the answer to this complement and the preposition used depends on the verb used and the place where the person or thing is located.

   A verb of state (**abitare, essere,** or **rimanere**)

would have a **complemento di stato in luogo** . It asks the question *where and in what place?*:

> Sono **a Roma**! Vieni a trovarmi?
>
> *I am **in Rome**! Are you coming to visit me?*

> Rimango **in Italia**: mi trovo bene qui.
>
> *I am staying **in Italy**: I get on well here.*

> Ora non posso parlare perché sono **dal medico**.
>
> *Now I can't talk because I'm **at the doctor's office**.*

3. movement: **complemento di moto a/da/per luogo** can be complicated depending on the question the complement answers (**di moto a, di moto da, e di moto per** / *in motion to, in motion from,* and *in motion through/by*). The answer determines the preposition you use:

> Sara è appena tornata **dal mare**.
>
> *Sara just got back **from the beach**.*

I fuggitivi sono passati **per questo sentiero**: le loro impronte sono ancora fresche.

The fugitives passed by this trail: their prints are still fresh.

Abbiamo deciso di fare una passeggiata **fra gli alberi.**

*We decided to talk a walk **through the trees.***

Vado **in Inghilterra** per Ferragosto. Vieni anche tu?

*I am going **to England** for Ferragosto. Are you coming, too?*

4. time (**di tempo determinato, continuato**): this complement answers the questions *when and in which moment* or *when and for how long*:

La lezione comincia **alle 9**!

*The lesson starts **at 9**!*

Ci conosciamo **da 4 anni.**

*We have known each other **for four years.***

5. material (**di materia**): this complement answers the question *what is it made out of it*:

> Quella brocca è **di vetro**, non **di plastica**.
>
> *That pitcher is **glass**, not **plastic**.*

6. subject or topic (**di argomento**): this complement answers the question *about what*:

> Oggi **discutiamo di politica**. Marco, ci parleresti della legge elettorale proposta dal governo in questi ultimi giorni?
>
> *Today let's **talk politics**. Marco, would you tell us about the electoral law proposed by the government in recent days?*

7. company or union (**di compagnia** o **di unione**): this complement answers the question *with whom* or *with what*:

> Vado **con Giulio** al teatro.
>
> *I am going **with Giulio** to the theater.*

> Viaggio sempre **con una valigia grande** da mettere in stiva.
>
> *I always travel **with a large bag** that has to be checked.*

8. possession (**di specificazione**): this complement answers the question *whose*:

> "Di chi è questo libro?"
>
> *Whose book is this?*
>
> È **di Marco**.
>
> *It's Marco's.*

9. denomination (**di denominazione**): this complement specifies the name of a place (although not always) by adding a further level of detail:

> Mi piacciono le chiese **di Roma**: c'è sempre qualcosa da scoprire tra questi edifici storici!
>
> *I like the churches of Rome: there is always something to discover among these historic buildings!*

10. partitive (**partitivo**): this complement expresses parts of a whole or particular items or people among a larger group of similar items/people. It asks *among who* or *what*. The preposition **di** is often employed or the prepositions **tra** or **fra:**

> Ho comprato **delle mele deliziose**. Ne vuoi una, per caso?
>
> *I bought some delicious apples. Would you like one by chance?*

> Uno **di voi** ha rotto la finesta. Chi è stato?
>
> *One **of you** broke the window? Who was it?*

11. agent (**d'agente o causa efficiente**): this complement is common in passive constructions (**da** + **agente**). In Italian, *agents* can be people (**l'agente**) or things (**la causa efficiente**). It asks the question *by whom* or *by what*:

> La torta è stata preparata **da Michele**. (**agente**)
>
> *The cake has been prepared **by Michele**.*

> Il tetto della casa venne distrutto **dalla furia dell'uragano**. (**causa efficiente**)
>
> *The roof of the house was destroyed **by the hurricane's fury**.*

12. cause (**di causa**): this complement asks the question *why* or *for what reason* (in other words, the cause):

> **Per il maltempo** le strade furono chiuse al traffico.
>
> ***Due to bad weather** the streets were closed to traffic.*

174

13. goal or aim (**di fine o scopo**): this complement expresses the goal, aim or purpose and asks the question *why* or *for what purpose?*:

> Queste carte **da gioco** sono professionali
>
> *These playing cards are professional ones.*
>
> (Cards for *what purpose?* For *playing* = **da gioco**)

14. means or instruments (**di mezzo o strumento**): this complement asks *by way of who* or *what*: who or what provided the means to make the action happen:

> Ho dovuto rompere la grata **con un piede di porco** per poter proseguire.
>
> *I had to break the gate with a crowbar in order to be able to pass.*

15. "the how" or in what way (**di modo o maniera**), this complement asks *how* or *in what way:*

> Carlo ha baciato la sua ragazza **con passione**!
>
> *Carlo kissed his girlfriend passionately!*

16. qualities (**di qualità**): this complement describes the qualities or characteristics of someone or something and asks the question *with which qualities or characteristics:*

> Tuo figlio è un ragazzo **di grande umiltà.**
>
> *Your son is an immensely humble guy.*

Conclusion
Conclusione

These complements are rarely mentioned in Italian language grammar guides and texts for English speakers. Knowing these complements, while seemingly daunting at first, is useful because it makes you *think* about the question that each complement asks. By knowing the question, you can give the correct answer using the correct preposition!

Many texts and guides avoid these topics because they know that people want to and expect to learn a language quickly. Most guides and books come up with schematic groupings to make learning easier and faster. These methods work well for beginners. As your Italian becomes more advanced, the *why* becomes just as important because it helps you avoid choosing the incorrect preposition.

For more advanced students, understanding these complements can help you to speak the "real" Italian this book hopes is conveyed.

Simple prepositions (**preposizioni semplici**) in Italian are outlined below with their possible translations. *Remember that the translations provided here are not exhaustive.* They are provided here only as a point of departure:

Simple prepositions
Preposizioni semplici

- **di:** can mean *of* or *by* when talking about authorship; can be used to convey possession (Quella macchina è **di** Giulio / *That car is Giulio's*); **di** is also used in the construction of the partitive (**partitivo**): **Vorrei comprare delle mele rosse** / *I would like to buy some red apples.*)

- **a:** can mean *in* or *to*, depending on the context; introduces indirect objects (**L'ho detto a Giulio** / *I told Giulio.*)

- **da:** can mean *from* or *to* when talking about going to a place; also used to introduce the agent in passive phrases (**La palla era stata lanciata da me** / *The ball was thrown by me.*)

- **in:** can mean *in* or *to,* depending on the context (**Vado in America per l'estate** / *I am going to America for the summer*). **In** is used with certain locations that end in -ia (**Maria, stasera andrò in birreria con Tiziano.** / *Maria, tonight I am going to the pub with Tiziano.*)

- **con:** can mean *with*; in some contexts it can also mean, *to*: **Maria è sposata con Marco.** / *Maria is married to Marco.*)

- **su:** can mean *on* or *about* (**Ho studiato due libri sulla musicologia italiana** / *I studied two books about Italian musicology.*)

- **per:** can mean *for* or *by,* depending on the context. (**Ho studiato per tre ore!** / *I studied for three hours!*)

- **fra/tra:** these two prepositions have the same meaning: *among, between,* or *in* with some time expressions. The choice between **fra/tra** is often dependent on the words that follow in order to avoid certain sound combinations (**Fra tutti i ragazzi tu sei quello più affascinante**. / *Among all the guys, you are the most fascinating one.*)

Palermo: Villa Bonanno (2014)

178

Articulated prepositions
Preposizioni articolate

Simple prepositions change form when combined with the definite article in Italian. This new form of the preposition is called **la preposizione articolata.** The chart below shows the various forms of the articulated prepositions:

	il	lo	l'	la	i	gli	le
a	al	allo	all'	alla	ai	agli	alle
con*	con il col	con lo collo	con l' coll'	con la colla	con i coi	con gli cogli	con le colle
da	dal	dallo	dall'	dalla	dai	dagli	dalle
di	del	dello	dell'	della	dei	degli	delle
in	nel	nello	nell'	nella	nei	negli	nelle
su	sul	sullo	sull'	sulla	sui	sugli	sulle

In writing the non-articulated form (con il, con la...**) is more often used; the articulated form is common in spoken Italian*

The prepositions **per, tra,** and **fra** do not combine with the definite article. **Con** can combine or remain separate.

In the next section we will profile the simple prepositions and some of their more common uses.

179

The preposition **di** is used in the following situations:

- to express possession:

> Questa penna è **della professoressa**: gliela restituirò domani a lezione.
>
> *This is the professor's pen: I will give it back to her in class tomorrow.*

- with certain expressions of time: **di mattina, di notte, d'estate, d'inverno,** and **del pomeriggio** (*in the morning, at night, in the summer, in the winter, in the afternoon*):

> **D'estate** è sempre meglio indossare gli abiti **di lino**: sono più leggeri e comodi!
>
> *In the summer, it is always better to wear linen clothing: they are lighter and more comfortable.*

Di is also used to describe what something is made out of (**di lino**).

- to express authorship:

> *Il giorno della civetta* **di Sciascia** è il mio libro preferito!
>
> *The Day of the Owl by Sciascia is my favorite book.*

Preposition, **di**
Preposizioni, di

• to express a topic or a subject of discussion:

> Quel giornalista scrive sempre **della chiesa e dei suoi problemi.**
>
> *That journalist always writes **about the church and its problems.***

Preposition, a
Preposizione, a

The preposition **a** in Italian, as we have noted, introduces our indirect object (**complemento di termine**). It is also used:

- to indicate a city or place where one is or is going:

> Quando ci siamo conosciuti, abitavo **a Londra**, ma adesso vivo **a Berlino**.
>
> *When we met each other, I was living in London, but now I am living in Berlin.*

- to indicate the distance needed to get from one place to another:

> Giulio, vuoi andare a trovare Marina? Abita **a 2 km** dai tuoi genitori.
>
> *Giulio, do you want to visit Marina? She lives 2 km from your parents'.*

- with certain improper prepositions, such as **vicino, sopra, davanti,** and **dietro**:

> Non mi piace quando una persona alta si siede **davanti a me** al cinema.
>
> *I don't like it when a tall person sits in front of me at the movies.*

- to express the exact time that something takes place:

> Sbrigati! Il film comincia **alle 21**!
>
> *Hurry up! The movie starts **at 9pm**!*

Preposition, **da**
Preposizione, da

The preposition **da** has many uses in Italian. The uses outlined below are commonly encountered. **Da** is used to:

- indicate a place where you are going, such as a friend's place (**dal mio amico**), the doctor's office (**dal medico**), the mechanic's (**dal meccanico**), to the zoo (**dallo zoo**), etc.:

> Devo portare quanto prima la macchina **da Franco**, il meccanico, perché quando l'accendo fa rumori strani.
>
> *I have to bring my car **to Franco**, the mechanic, as soon as possible because, when I turn it on, it makes strange noises.*

- express (with the present tense) an action that began in the past and continues to the present day (which you are still doing, i.e. *present perfect continuous*):

> Abito a Roma **da più di tre anni** e c'è sempre qualcosa di nuovo da scoprire!
>
> *I have been living in Rome **for more than 3 years**, and there is always something new to discover! (and still are living there)*

- indicate the age of someone when followed by a noun that coincides with certain periods of one's life:

> **Da bambino** mi piaceva giocare a calcio, ma da molti anni oramai non tocco più un pallone.
>
> *As a child I used to like to play soccer, but I haven't touched the ball for many years now.*

- indicate movement *from* a place:

> Quei rumori assordanti vengono **da quel maledetto locale**!
>
> *Those deafening noises are coming from that dang bar!*

- indicate the agent (**agente**) in passive constructions:

> Questo delizioso pranzo è stato offerto **dall'associazione** di cui faccio parte.
>
> *This delicious lunch has been offered by the association that I take part in.*

Preposition, in
Preposizione, in

The preposition **in** is similar to English, and many of its uses should be familiar. Some of the uses illustrated below are commonly encountered. **In** is used to:

- indicate a country, continent, or other geographical place that is *not* a city:

> Mia madre è imbranata: quando vuole chiamare qui **in Italia**, non solo sbaglia il prefisso, ma si dimentica persino del fuso orario!
>
> *My mom is a dolt: when she wants to call here* ***to Italy***, *not only does she get the prefix wrong but she even forgets about the time zone!*

Avviso!

When indicating places that one knows well (such as the home), or you refer to place in a general manner, use the simple preposition:

Mamma, ho messo le scarpe **in** balcone.	*Mom, I put the shoes on the balcony.*
In posti diversi ho sentito un gran caldo.	*I felt an intense heat in different places.*

To specify a particular place, use the articulated one:

Mamma ho messo le scarpe **nel** balcone della tua camera.
Mom, I put the shows on the balcony of your bedroom.

Nei posti che ho visitato ho sentito un gran caldo.
In places that I visited I felt an intense heat.

- indicate where you are going with certain places, such as **in casa**, places that end in **-ia (libreria, birreria, pizzeria)**, rooms in the home **(in cucina, in salotto)**, etc.:

> A Marco non piace andare fuori a cena **nei ristoranti**: preferisce andare **in pizzeria** non solo perché costa di meno, ma anche perché non sa fare la pizza in casa.
>
> *Marco doesn't like to go out to eat **in restaurants**: he prefers going **to the pizzeria** not only because it costs less, but also because he can't make pizza at home.*

- indicate the amount of time until an action is/was completed (note the difference between **in** and **tra/ fra**):

> Il professore si è complimentato con me: ho risposto a tutte le domande **in appena venti minuti**!
>
> *The teacher complimented me: I answered all the questions **in just 20 minutes**. (after 20 minutes passed, all the questions were answered)*

Preposition, **con**
Preposizione, con

The preposition **con** means *with* and is used:

- to express when things are *together*:

> Marco è rimasto senza mezzi, per cui verrà alla festa **con Nicola e Mariella.**
>
> *Marco was without any means of transport so he will come to the party **with Nicola and Mariella.***

Avviso!
It is important to understand the difference between **tra/fra** and **in** with expressions of time:

In conveys how much time it takes for an action *to be completed.*

Tra/fra conveys how much time must pass *before an action will take place.*

- with the verb **sposarsi (con)** to express *being married (to):*

> Gina è sposata **con Marco**, non **con Ruggiero!**
>
> *Gina is married to Marco, not (to) Ruggiero!*

- to describe how people or things are:

> La mia maglietta azzurra si sposa perfettamente **con i miei pantaloni beige.**
>
> *My blue shirt goes perfectly **with my beige pants.***

Preposition, su
Preposizione, su

The preposition **su** is used to:

- express topics or discussion points that a person (or thing) is talking *about*:

> In genere non mi piace guardare i documentari **sulla storia antica**, ma quello che ho visto l'altra sera era davvero interessante.
>
> *I usually don't like to watch documentaries **about ancient history**, but that one I saw the other evening was really interesting.*

- express where something is located or lies:

> "Mamma, dove hai messo le chiavi? Devo uscire!"
>
> *"Mom, where did you put the keys? I have to go out!"*
>
> "Santi numi, sono **su quel ripiano!**"
>
> *"Good Heavens, they are **on that shelf!**"*

Preposition, per
Preposizione, per

The preposition **per** has the following uses in Italian:

- with the verb **partire** to mean *to* or *for:*

> "Scusi, questo treno parte **per Milano?**"
>
> *"Excuse me, does this train go **to Milano?**"*
>
> "No, signora, questo parte **per Venezia.** Vada al binario 2, ma si sbrighi perché il treno è in partenza!"
>
> *"No, signora, this one goes **to Venice.** Go to track 2, but please hurry because the train is departing!"*

- with the verb **passare** to mean *by:*

> Siamo passati **per** quell'osteria che hai consigliato, ma è chiusa per ferie.
>
> *We passed **by** that osteria you recommended, but it is closed for vacation.*

- to express **in order to**:

> Vorrei andare un giorno in Australia, ma **per arrivare** lì ci vogliono ben venti ore di viaggio: non so se sarò in grado di resistere così a lungo!
>
> *I would like to go to Australia one day, but, it takes a good 20 hours of traveling **to get there**: I don't know if I will be able to resist so long!*

- in expressions of time, to say how long an action took place:

> Il terremoto durò **per più di cinque minuti**: è stata un'esperienza orribile!
>
> *The earthquake lasted **for more than 5 minutes**: it was a terrible experience!*

Preposition, **tra/fra**
Preposizione, tra/fra

The prepositions **tra** and **fra** mean the same in Italian. The choice usually depends on the words that come before. In Italian, it is common to avoid repeating the same sound: imagine how difficult it can be say (very fast) **tra tre ore!**

Tra and **fra** are used to:

- express being within a group of something. In English, we would say *among*:

> La foresta è così fitta che non si riesce a scorgere nulla **fra gli alberi.**
>
> *The forest is so thick that you can't spot anything among the trees.*

- express the location of something *between another thing*:

> "Marco, tu che vivi in questa zona: mi sai dire dove si trova l'ufficio postale?"
>
> *"Marco, since you live in this neighborhood: can you tell me where the post office is?"*
>
> "Non puoi sbagliarti: è proprio **tra la libreria e il supermercato!**"
>
> *"You can't go wrong: it is right between the bookstore and the supermarket!"*

- express how much time will pass before an action will begin:

> "Carlo, ti va di andarci a fare una passeggiata al parco più tardi?"
>
> *"Carlo, do you feel like going to take a walk in the park later?"*
>
> "Mi dispiace, ma non posso: **tra un'ora** devo accompagnare mamma dalla nonna."
>
> *"Sorry, but I can't: **in an hour** I have to go with my mom to my grandmother's house."*

Improper prepositions
Preposizioni improprie

As we mentioned earlier in the chapter, the second group of prepositions are known as **preposizioni improprie**. These are words that can function as other parts of speech. Keep in mind that many words in Italian have different functions. Being aware of when a word functions as a preposition or as an adjective will help you to be a better communicator.

dopo
after

Dopo means *after* in both time (**dopo la festa** / *after the party*) and space (**dopo il supermercato** / *after the supermarket*). Be careful because **dopo** can also function as a conjunction (**dopo che**) and an adverb. **Dopo** requires the preposition **di** before a pronoun (**dopo di me**) but not before a noun (**dopo Marco)**.

In the example below, you are talking to a friend of yours who is visiting from Scandinavia. You tell her that, after eating lunch, a short nap is in order:

> Mi capita spesso di concedermi una pennichella **dopo pranzo**.
>
> *I often get to have a nap after lunch.*

durante
during

Durante is a preposition that is derived from a verb (**durare**). It is used to express a duration. It can be translated as *during* or, in some time expressions, *for* (**durante un mese** / *for a month*):

> Sono solito leggere un libro **durante la pausa pranzo**: mi rilassa.
>
> *I am usually reading a book **during my lunch break**: it relaxes me.*

fuori
outside, out of

The preposition **fuori** can also be an adverb. **Attenzione:**. as an adverb, it means *out of* or *outside*. The preposition **di** is often placed between the preposition and noun. Also, the preposition **da** often comes between the two:

> Carola ha buttato **fuori (di) casa** suo marito: evidentemente le avrà fatto le corna!
>
> *Carola threw her husband **out of the house**: he will obviously have cheated on her!*

insieme
together

Insieme (or **assieme**) means *along/together (with)*. It is usually an adverb but becomes a preposition when used with the prepositions **a** or **con**:

> Stasera andrò al cinema **insieme al** (*or* **col**) mio **ragazzo**: spero non mi proponga uno dei suoi soliti film noiosi!
>
> *Today I will go to the movies **along with my boyfriend**: I hope he doesn't propose one of his usual boring films.*

presso
near, by, at

Presso has various meanings depending on its context. It is a synonym for **vicino (a)** (*near, nearby*), but it is also used in a business context to mean *at*:

> L'azienda **presso** cui lavoro è in forte crisi e ha licenziato molti dei miei colleghi.
>
> *The company that I work at is in a difficult position and has fired many of my colleagues.*

secondo
according to
in someone's opinion

Secondo is a useful preposition that means *according to* or *in someone's opinion*. You will often here expressions like **secondo me** or **secondo te** (*in my opinion, in your opinion*) spoken. Be careful: **secondo** can also be an adjective, noun, and even a conjunction:

> **Secondo alcuni studi recenti** il cioccolato fondente, se assunto quotidianamente in piccole dosi, può apportare benefici alla salute.
>
> *According to some recent studies, dark chocolate, if consumed daily in small doses, can bring benefits to one's health.*

senza
without

Senza means *without*. It can be used to express exclusivity, meaning *excluding* (**La stanza costa 40 euro senza la colazione** / The room costs 40 euro *excluding* breakfast) in some contexts. The preposition **di** can come before tonic pronouns:

> Nietzsche disse che **senza musica** la vita sarebbe un errore: come dargli torto!
>
> *Nietzsche said that **without music** life would be a mistake: how can anyone say he is wrong!*

vicino (a)
near, nearby

Vicino (a) means *near* or *nearby*. The preposition **a** is required before any noun or pronoun. As a preposition, **vicino** is **invariable.** Remember that **vicino** is both an adverb and an adjective. It is a preposition only when followed by the preposition **a:**

> "Salve! Sa dirmi se nei dintorni c'è una farmacia?"
>
> *"Hi, can you tell me if there is a pharmacy around?"*
>
> "Dovrebbe essercene una poco più avanti, **vicino a quell'incrocio.**"
>
> *"There should be one just a bit up ahead, **near the intersection.**"*

Locuzioni prepositive
Prepositional phrases

Locuzioni prepositive or *prepositional phrases* combine two or more words that take on the function of a preposition. The last word of the phrase is always a preposition. Here are some common prepositional phrases you should know:

a causa di
due to, because of

A causa di is a useful expression to know. Remember not to forget the **a** or **di** when using this expression. :

> Ho litigato con Irene **a causa di una divergenza di opinioni**.
>
> *I argued with Irene **because of a difference of opinion**.*

al di là di
beyond

Al di là di means *beyond*.

> Mi sono sempre chiesto cosa ci sia **al di là di quel recinto** che delimita la campagna dei miei nonni.
>
> *I have always asked myself what there was **beyond that fence** that marked off my grandparents' land.*

al pari di
equal to, like

Al pari di means *equal to* or *like*.

> Ti ho sempre considerato **al pari degli altri tuoi colleghi**, se non di più: abbi più fiducia in te stesso!
>
> *I always considered you **equal to some of your other colleagues**, if not more so: have more faith in yourself!*

a titolo di
as an, by way of, out of

The prepositional phrase **a titolo di** is an interesting expression that does not easily translate to English. Its meaning depends on the context in which it is used.

> Alla conferenza ho accennato agli studi condotti da una mia collega **a titolo di esempio**: non volevo certo prenderne i meriti!
>
> *At the conference, I touched on studies conducted by a colleague of mine **as an example**: I certainly didn't intend to take credit for them.*

Some other useful expressions with this preposition:
a titolo di amicizia = *for/out of friendship*
a titolo di curiosità = *out of curiousity*

(in) quanto a
as for, concerning, regarding

(In) quanto a means *as for, concerning,* or *regarding*:

> **(In) quanto al progetto del tram**, la città di Palermo presenta ancora molte problematiche: speriamo che il nuovo mezzo di trasporto venga attivato il prima possibile!
>
> ***Concerning the tram project**, the city of Palermo still presents many problems: let's hope that the new means of transport is set up as soon as possible.*

8 Conjunctions
Congiunzioni

In Italian, **conjunctions** are invariable parts of speech whose function is to combine two or more words or phrases. In English, they are words such as *and*, *but*, & *or*. In Italian, these same words exist and are important to learn because they allow for the construction of more elegant phrases.

In Italian, there are two types of *conjunctions*, **coordinanti** and **subordinanti** (*coordinating* and *subordinating*).

Types of Conjunctions
Tipi di congiunzioni

Congiunzioni coordinanti or *coordinating conjunctions* serve to connect two words or phrases that are considered grammatically equal. When they join two phrases, neither phrase depends on the other for meaning. Both phrases can exist on their own.

In Italian **congiunzioni coordinanti** can be:

- **copulative** (*copulative*): either affirmative or negative, depending on the phrase. Combines two words or phrases of similar 'value'.

- **avversative** (*adversative*): used to express a contrast.

- **disgiuntive** (*disjunctive*): expresses a separation between two phrases or possible options (For example: Vorresti un caffè **o** un the? / *Do you want coffee or tea?* -- you can only choose one or the other).

- **dichiarative** (or **esplicative**) (*declarative* or *explanative*): these conjunctions express a declaration or explanation.

- **conclusive** (*conclusive*): indicates a conclusion or a consequence; in other words, one thing took place, leading to another.

- **correlative** (*correlative*): they come in pairs and act as 'stabilizers' by connecting two words or phrases.

Congiunzioni subordinanti or *subordinating conjunctions* serve to connect two words or phrases that are not grammatically equal. In other words, one phrase is *subordinate* to the other for meaning.

In Italian, **congiunzioni subordinanti** can be:

- **dichiarative** (*declarative*): these conjunctions express a declaration or explanation.

- **condizionali** (*conditional*): used to indicate a condition.

- **causali** (*causal*) : used to indicate a cause, reason or motive.

- **finali** (*final*): used to indicate the purpose or an aim (**Ti ho dato il libro perché tu potessi studiare per l'esame.** / *I gave you the book so that you could study for the exam.*)

- **concessive** (*concessive*): used to contrast one idea with another, where one of the ideas is unusual or surprising (**Benché avessi studiato per tre settimane, non avevo superato l'esame.** / *Even though I had studied for three weeks, I still did not pass the exam*).

- **consecutive** (*consecutive*): expresses the consequences of the action of the independent clauses (**Ho bevuto così tanta birra che ho perso i sensi** / *I drank so much beer that I passed out*).

- **temporali** (*temporal*): expresses *when* (**Devi fare la doccia prima che tu vada a letto** / *You have to take a shower before you go to bed*).

- **comparative** (*comparative*): used to express a majority, a minority or equality.

- **modali** (*modal*): used to express the way an action is expressed (in other words, *how*).

- **avversative** (*adversative*): used to express a contrast.

- **esclusive** (*exclusive*): used to indicate an exception or limitation to what is stated in the independent clause (implicit: **Dario passa tutta la giornata in ufficio senza muovere un dito!** or explicit: **Dario passa tutta la giornata in ufficio senza che muova un dito!** / *Dario spent all day at the office without lifting a finger!*).

It is important to keep in mind that some conjunctions have two roles. **Quando**, for example, means *when* but can also be **avversativa** and **temporale**. When in doubt, consult a good dictionary for help!

Within each type of conjunction (**coordinanti** and **subordinanti**), there are various subtypes (*copulative, avversative,* etc.). Some of the most important and common conjunctions will be explored in this chapter.

Conjunctions in Italian can be:

1. **semplici** or *simple:* made up of only one word (**però**)

2. **composte** or *compound:* made up of two or more words that are not separated (**perché**)

3. **locuzioni congiuntive** or *conjunctive phrases:* made up of two or more separate words (**anche se**)

affinché
so that, in order that

Affinché is a subordinating conjunction (**finale**) that expresses a finality or an end to something. The subjunctive (**congiuntivo**) always follows this conjunction. The conjunction **perché** is synonymous with **affinché**, and it too requires the subjunctive. Don't forget that when **perché** is followed by the indicative, it is a **congiunzione causale** and means *because*.

While on the train, a young woman was complaining about her Latin teacher because he was too strict and assigned too much work. Her friend said that this was a good thing, remarking about her own experiences:

> Il nostro professore di latino era davvero severo con noi: più tardi capimmo che si comportava così **affinché** studiassimo con più diligenza e serietà.
>
> *Our Latin teacher was really strict with us: later we realized that he behaved in this way **so that** we would study more seriously and diligently.*

anche & neanche
also, even, too, as well
&
even

Anche and **neanche** are **congiunzioni copulative** (**affirmative** and **negative**, respectively). **Neanche** can also be an adverb. **Anche** means *also*, *too*, and *as well*. It can also translate to *even*. As a conjunction, **neanche** means *even* and is used in negative phrases.

Imagine you just had some work done on your car last week. You are talking with a friend about the fact that your car is still giving you trouble:

> **Anche** avendo fatto la revisione la settimana scorsa, la mia macchina continua ad avere problemi al quadro elettrico.
>
> *Even after having the service done last week, my car continues to have problems with the electrical panel.*

Anche can be combined with the preposition **se** to create a compound conjunction that is often used to express concessive hypotheticals (***Even if*** *I had the money, I couldn't have gone on vacation. I just have too much to do at the office!*). Your girlfriend is upset with you because you do not want to go with her to the mall. You try to smooth things over by inviting her to the soccer match, but she replies:

> **Anche se** mi piacesse il calcio, non andrei mai allo stadio con te!
>
> *Even if I liked soccer, I would never go with you to the stadium!*

Neanche means *even*, but it is used in a variety of idiomatic expressions as a conjunction. You just got off the phone with your friend, Alessandra. You asked her about Marco, who has not been seen for ages. As you round the corner to descend into the metro station, you see Marco coming up the stairs. You remark:

> **Neanche** a farlo apposta, appena ho chiesto di te, mi sei apparso dinanzi qualche istante dopo.
>
> *As luck would have it, as soon as I asked about you, you appeared in front of me moments after.*

che
that

Che is a subordinating conjunction that wears many hats in Italian. Not only is it a relative pronoun, but it is also a conjunction with a variety of roles. One of the most common is its function as a **congiunzione dichiarativa** (*declarative conjunction*) meaning *that*. In some contexts, it can also mean *because*, *until*, and much more. Not all uses of **che** can be easily translated into English. For the sake of simplicity, we shall focus on **che** as a *declarative conjunction*.

I have a friend here in Italy who was unsure if he should take the entrance exam for medical school. He had some doubts. I told him that he should pursue it because he had a knack for science and working with people:

> Sono dell'idea **che** tu debba provare ad entrare a medicina: sei portato per questo mestiere!
>
> *I think (**that**) you should try to go into medicine: you have a natural talent for this career!*

In English (as you can see above) *that* is often omitted. In Italian, it almost always required unless used with verbs of thinking or believing (**sperare, credere, pensare,** etc.).

> Spero vivamente (**che**) tu possa guarire in breve tempo.
>
> *I strongly hope (**that**) you can heal in a short time!*

Attenzione! Che *cannot* be omitted when it is used as a relative pronoun!

As you can see from these two examples, **che** is often a sign that the *subjunctive* (**congiuntivo**) needs to be employed. The expression **essere dell'idea** requires the subjunctive as does the verb **sperare**. See the grammar note at the end of this chapter on the subjunctive.

dal momento che
dato che
visto che
since

The conjunctions **dal momento che, dato che,** and **visto che** are known as **locuzioni congiuntive** (*conjunctive phrases*). They collectively mean *since*.

Dato che can also be translated as *given that,* and **visto che** can also mean *seeing that.* These three are *subordinating conjunctions* and are *causal* (**causali**). All three can be used interchangeably.

Have you ever planned an evening out with friends? You know how hard it can be at times to find a place that everyone likes. It is not easy to find a great sushi place in Italy. When you do, it can be quite an event, although not everyone is a fan:

> **Dato che** non ama il pesce, Fabiola ha deciso di non venire con noi a mangiare del sushi.
>
> *Since she doesn't like fish, Fabiola decided not to come with us to have some sushi*

ma & però
but

Ma and **però** are both **congiunzioni coordinanti** (*coordinating conjunctions*). Both are **avversative** (*adversative*) and indicate a contrast.

Ma can be used when you want to add some emphasis (**Ma che cavolo vuole?**) and can also be used conclusively (**Ma comunque non voglio parlarne più, è chiaro?**). **Ma** *always* comes at the beginning of the dependent clause.

Però, on the other hand, is only used adversatively and is considered more emphatic than **ma.** However, its position in the phrase can shift and does not have to come at the beginning of the phrase (see the example below). **Però** is also preferred in formal writing.

In spoken Italian, **però** was often used with **ma (ma però)** to add further emphasis to the contrast. *This usage should be avoided!*

Last month I was in Palermo, and the great Bahrami was performing. I asked my friend, Francesco, if he wanted to go, but, after weeks of exams, he was just too tired:

> "Francesco, ti va di andare a teatro? Suona il grande Bahrami!"
>
> *"Francesco, do you feel like going to the theatre? The great Bahrami is playing!"*
>
> "Sai benissimo che adoro come suona, **ma** sono davvero stanco...mi dispiace!"
>
> *or*
>
> "Sai benissimo che adoro come suona, **però***** sono (**però**) davvero stanco (**però**)...mi dispiace!"
>
> *"You well know that I adore how he plays, **but** I am really too tired...I'm sorry!"*

In the example above, **però can be placed in any of the positions identified. It would not appear three times in the phrase.*

malgrado
nonostante
though, although

Malgrado and **nonostante** are both **congiunzioni subordinanti** and **concessive** (*concessive subordinating conjunctions*). They require the subjunctive. In English, they mean *though* or *although*.

If you spend any time in Rome or any other Italian cities, you will notice that, when it rains, the streets often become 'canals' and make driving difficult! I remember talking to a friend about a drive home this winter with a mutual friend of ours. We talked about how the weather took a turn for the worst during that trip home. I remarked:

> Sono riuscito a raggiungere la città, **malgrado*** le condizioni atmosferiche fossero peggiorate e la macchina avesse dei problemi al motore.
>
> *I was able to reach the city, **although** weather conditions had worsened, and the car had some problems with the motor.*

In the phrase above, you could substitute **malgrado with* **nonostante**.

perché
because
so that

Perché is a subordinating conjunction (**congiunzione subordinante**) and translates as *because*. When it is used *causally*, it is followed by the *indicative* (**indicativo**):

> Non sono andato al compleanno di Valeria, **perché** non c'è alcun dubbio che mi sarei annoiato a morte!
>
> *I didn't go to Valeria's birthday **because** there is no doubt I would have been bored to death.*

When it is used as a *final conjunction* (**finale**), it is a synonym for **affinché** and means *so that*. It must be followed by the *subjunctive* (**congiuntivo**).

Perché is also used as an *interrogative conjunction*.

pure
even

Pure means *even, even though, yet,* and *but*. It is a *coordinating adversative conjunction* (**congiunzione coordinante e avversativa**). As an adversative conjunction (**eppure = e pure**), it means *yet* or *but*. It can also reinforce other conjunctions, such as **tuttavia** or **nondimeno**:

> Non c'è un filo di vento, **eppure** oggi si sta bene fuori casa.
>
> *There isn't a breath of wind, **yet** today you can be comfortable outdoors.*

Its concessive usage (meaning: *even, even though*) is used when it precedes implicit constructions (where the subject is implied and not stated) such as with the **gerundio** (where **pure** is often truncated to **pur**).

Imagine you have a friend who has mistreated you. Your friend is unwilling to admit her error, and, in recounting the tale to another friend, you remark:

> **Pur** sapendo in cuor suo di aver sbagliato, Irene non vuole in alcun modo fare il primo passo per recuperare la nostra amicizia.
>
> *Even knowing in her heart that she is wrong, Irene does not want to make the first move in any way to salvage our friendship.*

Pur di is a conjunction that means *in order to*. It can have a final or conditional meaning. Remember that **congiunzioni finali** (*final conjunctions*) communicate a purpose or an aim (see below). **Pur di** is a common construction in Italian, and you will see it quite often.

Imagine your son has been complaining for weeks about his homework and teachers. Today, he is complaining about feeling under the weather. You let him stay home and explain to your friend the reasons:

> **Pur di** non andare a scuola, mio figlio si è preso il raffreddore.
>
> *My son caught a cold **in order to** skip to school.*

se
if

Se translates as *if* and is a *subordinating conjunction* that is most often *conditional* (**condizionale**). **Se** can also be *causal* and *interrogative* depending on the context. **Se** is renowned for being a popular 'foil' for many students of Italian because it is how hypotheticals are formed (see the grammar note at the end of this chapter for more on hypothetical constructions). When **se** introduces a possible or unreal hypothetical situation, it requires the subjunctive, *not* the conditional.

Imagine that you have just failed one of your oral exams. You start to have doubts and wonder if things might not have gone different *if*...

> Da giorni mi chiedo: **se** fossi andato al ricevimento dal professore per mostrarmi interessato alla sua materia, mi avrebbe fatto superare l'esame senza mettermi in difficoltà?
>
> *I have been asking myself for days: **if** I had gone to the professor's office hours to show I was interested in the material, would he have let me pass the exam without giving me any trouble?*

sia...sia
both...and

Sia...sia is a *correlative conjunction* (**congiunzione correlativa**) and usually used in pairs. It translates into English as *both...and*. It can have disjunctive properties and then translate as *whether...or*. This correlative conjunction is common in writing, and you will see it a lot. Don't confuse it with the first, second and third person present subjunctive of **essere**!

Your friend, Federica, invited you to a singing competition at her university. She was up against some tough competition, and, in the end, she lost to someone who was slightly better. You recount to your mutual friend, Stefania, what transpired and why Federica lost:

Al concorso di canto hanno dato il primo premio a Claudio piuttosto che a Federica **sia** per la sua tecnica vocale superiore **sia** per la coinvolgente presenza scenica.

*At the song competition, they gave first prize to Claudio instead of to Francesca **both** for his superior vocal technique **and** for his engrossing stage presence.*

Milano: Stazione Centrale (2014)

Il periodo ipotetico or *hypothetical phrases* in Italian can be confusing. In Italian, they are formed with the conjunction **se.**

The **se** *clause* is known as the **ipotesi** or the *hypothesis*. The independent clause that follows is known as the **conseguenza** or *consequence*. The order of the two phrases is unimportant. However, when the **se** *clause* comes *after* the consequence, it *is not* separated by a comma.

There are four main hypothetical situations with **se** *clauses*. They are described below with the necessary 'formula' for constructing them correctly:

1. *real*

   se + **indicativo presente, indicativo presente**
   se + **indicativo presente, imperativo**
   se + **indicativo presente, futuro**
   se + **futuro, futuro**

2. **a)** *possible but difficult to make happen* or **b)** *unreal and impossible to make happen in the present or future*

   se + **congiuntivo imperfetto, condizionale presente**

3. *unreality, referring to something in the past which never had the chance of happening*

   se + **congiuntivo trapassato, condizionale passato**

continued...

real:

Se **ho** tempo, ti **aiuto** con i compiti.
If I have time, I will help you with your homework.

Porta un ombrello se **piove**.
Bring an umbrella if it rains.
  nb: note the placement of the *se* clause and no comma!

Se tua madre non **sta** bene, **chiamerai** il medico.
If your mother is not well, you will call the doctor.

Se mio padre non **lavorerà** domani, **andrò** al cinema.
If my father isn't working tomorrow, I will go to the movies.

possible but difficult to make happen or *unreal and impossible to make happen in the present or future*:

Se **fossi** a casa, **guarderei** la partita. Purtroppo, sono fuori!
If I were at home, I would watch the match. Unfortunately, I'm out!

Se **fossi** ricco, **comprerei** una casa a Londra e New York.
If I were rich, I would buy a house in London and New York.

unreal, referring to something in the past which never had the chance to happen:

Se **avesse comprato** l'altra casa, **saremmo stati** più felici.
If he had bought the other house, we would have been happier.

The conjunction **che** often requires *the subjunctive* (**il congiuntivo**) after verbs of *emotion, uncertainty*, certain *impersonal expressions,* etc. The indicative (**indicativo**) is the mood which conveys certainty, whereas the subjunctive (**congiuntivo**) is the mood which conveys *doubt, impossibility* and *opinions*.

1. The following verbs require the subjunctive:

avere paura *to be afraid*	**credere** *to believe*	**desiderare** *to desire*
immaginare *to imagine*	**pensare** *to think*	**preferire** *to prefer*
sperare *to hope*	**temere** *to fear*	**volere** *to want*

Voglio che tu mi **dica** la verità!
I want you to tell me the truth!

Speriamo lei non **diventi** un problema.
Let's hope she doesn't become a problem.

2. Impersonal expressions also require the subjunctive (also in the negative):

non è certo che*	*it is not certain that...*	(see point #7)
(non) è giusto che	*it is right...*	
(non) è importante che	*it is important that...*	
(non) è intelligente che	*it is intelligent that...*	
(non) è meglio che	*it is better that...*	
(non) è probabile che	*it is probable that...*	
(non) è strano che	*it is strange that...*	

Non è strano che Maria **sia venuta** alla festa senza Marco?
It isn't strange that Maria came to the party without Marco?

È meglio che vadano dal medico di mattina.
It is better that they go to the doctor's in the morning   *continued...*

3. The subjunctive is required after the relative superlative (**il superlativo relativo**):

Maria è **la ragazza più gentile** che **io abbia** mai **conosciuto**!
Maria is the nicest girl I have ever met!

4. The subjunctive is required after the following conjunctions: **benché, malgrado, nonostante, sebbene, affinché, qualora, purché, perché** (when it means *so that*), **nel caso che, a patto che, prima che:**

Prima che me ne vada, dammi un altro bicchiere di caffè!
Before I head out, give me another cup of coffee!

5. The subjunctive is also required after indefinite adjectives, pronouns and adverbs (such as **ovunque, qualunque, chiunque**, etc.):

Si mette nei guai **ovunque** vada!
He gets into trouble wherever he goes!

Chiunque abbia qualcosa da ridire, lo faccia adesso o mai più!
Whoever has something to say again, do it now or never again!

Andrò avanti lo stesso, **qualunque siano** le difficoltà da affrontare!
I will go forward anyway, whatever difficulties there may be to face.

Remember the subjunctive is not used:

6. If the subjects of both the independent & dependent clauses are the same, the phrase remains in the indicative and the preposition,**di** is used in place of **che**:

continued...

Antonio, vai alla festa di Marco stasera?
Antonio, are you going to Marco's party tonight?

No, **non credo di** andare: sono molto stanco.
No, I don't believe I am going: I'm very tired.

7. If the verb or impersonal expression in the independent clause communicates certainty:

È ovvio che ti ha tradito!
It is obvious that he betrayed you!

È certo che* non ho intenzione di sedermi in macchina accanto a te!
I certainly have no intention of sitting next to you in the car!

9 Interjections
Interiezioni

Interjections (or exclamations) are words or phrases that are used to convey emotions or feelings, such as pain, pleasure, surprise, etc. In English, words like *Oops* or *Dang* are common interjections as are greetings and salutations, such as *Hi* and *Bye*.

These same words exist in Italian, and, as you make your way around any Italian city or town, you are bound to hear them. They are used a lot in spoken Italian, and it is important to learn them because they add a layer of understanding to conversations. In Italian, **le interiezioni** are classified into three basic types:*

1. proper (**proprie**) : these are words in Italian that function only as interjections and serve as no other part of speech (**Ahi! Boh! Uffa!**)

2. improper (**improprie**) : these are words in Italian that function as interjections but can also function as other parts of speech

- **Bravo!** (*Well done!*) : an adjective that can function as an interjection

- **Basta!** (*Enough*) : from the verb, **bastare**

- **Mostro!** (*Monster!* or *Fiend!*) : from the noun, **il mostro**

3. phrasal (**locuzioni**) : these are small groupings of words that act as interjections (**Mio Dio! Povero me! Porca miseria!**)

*There are other forms of interjections, such as **onomatopee** that imitate animal sounds (**miao**) or someone knocking on the door (**toc toc**). Greetings and salutations are also considered interjections (**Ciao, Buongiorno, Buondì,** etc.).*

Uses
Usi

In Italian, a simple interjection can often convey the same meaning as a longer phrase. They can be just as powerful and potent. Take for example the interjection **basta**. Imagine your children are fighting, and you want them to stop. You could shout:

Smettete di litigare!

Stop fighting!

Or, you could simply shout:

Basta!

Enough!

In the remainder of this section, some common interjections will be profiled. Try to use them in your speaking as these words tend to add color and variation to your Italian.

Remember that some of them do not translate easily from Italian to English, but their presence in the phrase can say a lot about how you are feeling and what you might be thinking.

auguri
congratulations, best wishes

This interjection comes from the noun **l'augurio**. It means *Congratulations* or *Best wishes*, It is used for birthdays, the birth of a child or some other achievement or recent success.

Your Italian friend will say to you on your birthday:

> Oggi è il tuo compleanno? Allora tanti **auguri**!
>
> *Today is your birthday? **Congratulations** then!*

basta
enough

As already mentioned, the interjection **basta** comes from the verb **bastare**. It means *Enough!* Imagine you have been a life-long smoker and have decided from this point forward you will not smoke another cigarette. You might say to yourself:

> **Basta!** Da oggi ho deciso che non fumerò più alcuna sigaretta.
>
> ***Enough!** Starting today I have decided I will not smoke anymore cigarettes.*

boh
dunno, who knows

Boh is a proper interjection (**interiezione propria**) that means *Dunno* or *Who knows*. It is used to express doubt and uncertainty. You might respond with **Boh** if your mother is always asking you where your brother has run off to:

> "Samuele, sai dov'è andato tuo fratello?"
>
> *"Samuele, do you know where you brother went?"*
>
> "**Boh!** Come al solito esce senza dire nulla."
>
> *"**Dunno!** As usual he left without saying anything."*

capperi
gosh, my word

As you have already guessed, the interjection **capperi** comes from the noun **cappero** (*capers*). The interjection means *Gosh* or *My word*. It is an interjection used to convey surprise. This interjection is a substitute for more off color interjections and swears (**parolacce**) you might be more inclined to hear.

In the example below, imagine you and your wife have traveled to a small **agriturismo** in the Sicilian countryside. You have finally arrived after hours on planes, trains, and automobiles. Your host asks where you are from, and you remark that you have traveled all the way from Calgary, Canada. Your host might say:

> **Capperi!** Certo che ne avete fatta di strada per arrivare fin qui.
>
> *My gosh! You certainly have come a long way to get to here.*

cavolo
gosh, damn

Cavolo is another noun that is often used as an interjection. It means *cabbage* but, as an interjection, means *Gosh*. It is used to express surprise. It can also mean *Damn* to express ire. Like the interjection **capperi**, **cavolo** is a more polite form of expressing ire or surprise. The example below shows how you might respond if you were on your way to work and realized you had left your keys at home once again:

> **Cavolo!** Ho dimenticato per l'ennesima volta le chiavi a casa!
>
> **Damn!** *I forget my keys for the umpteenth time at home!*

mah
you know!
who knows?

Mah is often used to express *uncertainty, bitterness* or *resignation* about something. It does not always translate easily into English. In English, we might say *You know (resignation)* or perhaps *Who knows (uncertainty)*. Consider this conversation below between two friends, discussing one of their recent trips to the post office:

> "Stamane sono andato alle poste e dopo ore di attesa non era più possibile pagare i bollettini per un guasto ai sistemi informatici!"
>
> *"This morning I went to the post office, and, after hours of waiting, it wasn't possible anymore to pay bills due to a breakdown of the computer systems!"*
>
> "**Mah**! È sempre la stessa storia: le nostre poste sono a dir poco imbarazzanti!"
>
> *"You know! It is always the same story: our post offices are embarrassing to say the least!"*

magari
if only, I wish

Magari has a number of roles in Italian and also functions as an adverb and a conjunction. When used as an interjection, it is often followed by the imperfect subjunctive (**congiuntivo imperfetto**) with the meaning *If only*. It can also mean *I wish...* as a response on its own to a question (Hai vinto la lotteria? - **Magari**!) or express a willingness for something or to do something (Vorresti una birra? - **Magari**!).

Imagine your best friend, Franco, has a thing for a young woman, Sabina, in his literature class. He wants to ask her out but cannot find the courage to ask he. He might say:

> **Magari** riuscissi a vincere la mia timidezza e a invitare Sabina a cena...
>
> *If only I could overcome my shyness and invite Sabina to dinner...*

uffa
bother, phew

Uffa is used to express *bother*, *impatience*, or *boredom*. It is also used to convey a sense of displeasure in extreme heat (**Uffa, che caldo!**). In English, we might translate this as *Bother* or *Phew*:

> **Uffa!** Piove a dirotto e non c'è nulla di interessante da fare!
>
> *Phew! It is pouring down, and there is nothing interesting to do!*

zitto
be quiet, shut up

Zitto is an adjective and agrees with the person or persons that you wish would be quiet. As an interjection, **zitto** must still agree with person or people that this interjection is directed at (so take note when using this expression).

It translates as *Be quiet* or *Shut up*. This expression is very strong and colloquial so only use it with people you know well. Using it with the wrong person can be very discourteous and rude. It is better to use the interjection **Silenzio** which strangers.

I remember going to the opera in Palermo earlier this year, and the three women I was sharing the box with were talking incessantly. During the first act. I kindly asked them several times to stop talking. Finally, I said:

> **Silenzio,** per piacere! Non si può parlare ad alta voce!
>
> *Be quiet, please! You cannot talk aloud!*

Zitto is often preceded by the verb **stare** in the **imperativo** (*imperative*), but it is often used on its own without the verb.

I remember when my friend, Carlo, was trying to take a phone call, and our friend, Stefania, would not stop talking! He shouted:

> (Stai) **Zitta!** Non lo vedi che sto parlando al telefono?!
>
> *Be quiet! Can't you see I am talking on the phone?!*

Palermo: Teatro Massimo, interior (2014)

10 Idioms
Modi di dire

This chapter will highlight useful idiomatic expressions or **modi di dire** that are common in Italian. These phrases and expressions were selected because I have encountered or heard them used here in Italy.

Many of these expressions are related to the body, animals, sports as well as religion and other aspects of Italian culture.

This chapter will be organized into the following sections:

- modi di dire that reference *animals*

- modi di dire that reference *the human body*

- modi di dire that reference *sports and games*

Idioms: animals
Modi di dire: gli animali

These idiomatic expressions are related to animals. Some of these expressions do not have direct equivalents in English, so their translations are *rough* or *approximate*. Study the context presented since this will help you understand not only the meaning but how these expressions are used.

essere una capra
to be ignorant; to not understand anything

The expression **essere una capra** literally means *to be a goat*. In Italian, being called *a goat* is not usually a compliment. This expression is used to describe someone who is ignorant or is unable to understand something.

American students get a lot of flack for knowing little about geography, but, at a party here in Rome, I heard some teachers talking about their students. One of them remarked:

> I miei alunni **sono** proprio **delle capre**: non sapevano che la Polonia è uno stato europeo!
>
> *My students **are really ignorant**: they didn't know that Poland is a European country!*

fare da cavia
to be the guinea pig

Fare da cavia means *to be a guinea pig*. In English, we use this expression when someone is doing something for the first time in order to see how something turns out. In Italian, the meaning is the same. How many times has one of us been asked to test out a teacher's classroom materials in front of the class?

> All'università il professore ha deciso di farmi **fare da cavia** per l'esercitazione in classe.
>
> *At university the professor had me **be the guinea pig** for the in class exercises.*

buttarsi a pesce (su qualcosa)
to throw oneself (at something)

The expression **buttarsi a pesce (su + qualcosa)** means *to throw oneself (at something)*. It literally means *to throw onself down like a fish*.

I always dread taking the Metro (underground) in Rome with my friend, Carlo, because he hates standing for long intervals and prefers to find an empty spot to sit down. Heaven help anyone who gets in his way once a spot opens up!

> Liberatosi un posto, Carlo **si buttò a pesce** per occuparlo.
>
> *With a space freed up, Carlo **threw himself** in order to occupy it.*

(qui) gatta ci cova
there's something fishy going on here

This is a cute expression I learned while putting the book together. I had never heard it before and wanted to share it with all of you. It is the expression **gatta ci cova** (it is sometimes used with the adverb, **qui**) and means *there's something fishy going on (here)*.

Imagine that you have two friends, Marco and Stefania. Both dating other people and *seem* to be spending a lot of time together. You might say to your friends:

> Marco e Stefania si vedono un po' troppo spesso: secondo me, **qui gatta ci cova**!
>
> *Marco and Stefania see each other a bit too often: in my opinion, **there's something fishy going on there**!*

in bocca al lupo
good luck!

This phrase confuses students of Italian to no end. I always get asked what this means and why Italians say it. The wolf is an important symbol for Italy. Rome was founded by Romulus and Remus, who were raised by a she-wolf. The origins of the phrase, though, are somewhat in dispute.

It is important to remember that when you want to wish someone *good luck* for something that they are about to undertake, such as an exam, a performance, or a difficult task, you say **in bocca al lupo**! Since a lot of Italians are superstitious (**scaramantico**), almost everyone will respond quickly with a **Crepi (il lupo)!** (*May the wolf perish!*)

> "Domani darò l'ultima materia all'università!"
>
> *"Tomorrow I will take my last subject at university!"*
>
> "Oramai sei ad un passo dalla laurea. **In bocca al lupo**, dunque!"
>
> *"Now you are one step from graduating. Well, **good luck!**"*
>
> "**Crepi!**"
>
> *"Thanks!"*

There are variants to this! There is the more colorful expression **in culo alla balena** (*in the ass of the whale*) to which one would respond **speriamo che non caghi** (*let's hope it doesn't shit*). It is also useful to point out that stepping on *dog doo-doo* in Italy is also considered good luck!

Firenze: Francesco con una statua di un cane al Giardino Bardini (2014)

fare una vita da cani
to live a dog's life

This expression **fare una vita da cani** means *to live a dog's life*. In English, the expression can be both positive or negative, depending on the context. However, the poor Italian dog is not living the high life its American and English counterparts seem to be living. In Italian the expression is only used with its negative context to refer to a life that is *miserable* and *difficult*.

> Francesco **fa una vita da cani**: è costretto a svegliarsi presto di mattina e lavora senza sosta fino a tarda sera; il tutto per uno stipendio misero.
>
> *Francesco **lives a dog's life**: he is forced to wake up early in the morning and work without stopping until late in the evening; all of this for a miserable wage.*

essere solo come un cane
to be all alone

The dogs are just not having any luck in Italian, are they? The expression **essere solo come un cane** means *to be all alone* (*literally: to be alone like a dog*):

> Andrea passa le giornate chiuso in casa, senza stare in contatto con nessuno: **è solo come un cane**!
>
> *Andrea spends days closed up at home without being in contact with anyone: **he is all alone**!*

il colpo di coda
sudden reversal

The expression **colpo di coda** means *sudden reversal*. Literally, it means a *strike of the tail*.

Le giornate torride delle settimane scorse sono state **il colpo di coda** di un'estate oramai agli sgoccioli, che cede il posto all'autunno.

*The sweltering days in the last weeks were a **sudden reversal** of a summer that, now coming to an end, is giving way to autumn.*

Idioms: human body
Modi di dire: il corpo

Expressions relating to the human body can be very useful to know in Italian. Some of them are equivalent to their English counterparts while others are rooted in Italian culture. When translated literally, they sometimes make little sense in English. This section will look at some of the common expressions that you have probably never encountered!

culo e camicia
*thick as thieves
hand in glove*

The expression **culo e camicia** means *thick as thieves* or *hand in glove*. It is used to describe two people who spend a lot of time together or are inseparable! The expression literally means *bum and shirt* and presumably refers to the closeness of one's shirttails to one's bum when getting dressed!

> Mario e Serena stanno sempre insieme, dalla mattina alla sera: sono proprio **culo e camicia**!
>
> *Mario and Serena are always together, from morning until evening: they are **as thick as thieves**!*

avere culo
to be lucky

This expression means *to be lucky* but literally means *to have some bum*. The noun **culo** can be modified by adjectives (as in our example below) to add emphasis! You might also hear the exclamation, **che culo**, which means *you lucky dog* or *what luck you have!*

> Il mio collega ha vinto alla lotteria: **ha avuto un culo incredibile**!
>
> *My colleague won the lottery: **he was incredibly lucky**!*

ad occhio e croce
roughly (speaking),
more or less

This expression **ad occhio e croce** means *roughly (speaking)* or *more or less*. It literally means *to the eye and cross*. It means you estimated something (a distance, a judgment, or a measurement) using only your eyes to get some form of approximation by running your gaze along two lines, one lengthwise and one for the width (much like the shape of the cross). The expression is believed to have come from the jargon used by silk weavers:

> **Ad occhio e croce** quel bambino avrà non più di dodici anni.
>
> *Roughly speaking, that child will not be older than 12 years old.*

portare
i pantaloni
to wear
the pants

The expression, **portare i pantaloni**, means *to wear the pants* or *to wear the trousers*. It refers to someone who makes the decisions and has the authority:

> Nella mia famiglia è mia madre a **portare i pantaloni**, per il suo carattere forte e a volte autoritario.
>
> *In my family, it is my mother who wears the pants due to her strong and, at times, authoritarian nature.*

avere un buco allo
stomaco
to have the munchies

Avere un buco allo stomaco means *to have the munchies*. It literally means *to have a hole in one's stomach*.

A causa del lavoro ho saltato il pranzo, e adesso **ho un buco allo stomaco**: non vedo l'ora di mangiare!

*Because of work I skipped lunch, and now **I have the munchies**: I can't wait to eat!*

avere (del) fegato
to have (some) guts; to have some nerve

The expression **avere (del) fegato** means *to have guts* or *to have some nerve*. It literally means *to have (some) liver*. It describes someone who has a lot of courage when facing difficult or nerve-racking situations (such as *bungee jumping*). In ancient times, the liver was believed to be the center of strength and power within the human body:

Il *bungee jumping* è una di quelle attività sportive "estreme" per le quali è necessario **avere del fegato** per praticarle.

*Bungee jumping is one of those extreme sport activities where it is necessary **to have some guts** to do it.*

restare/rimanere in mutande
to lose one's shirt

Restare or **rimanere in mutande** means *to lose one's shirt* or *to lose everything*. It literally means *to be in one's underwear*. It refers to someone who has lost everything that they have:

Il povero Claudio è **rimasto in mutande**: ha perso tutto a causa di un'ingente truffa, nella quale è stato inconsapevolmente coinvolto.

*Poor Claudio **lost everything**: he lost it all because of a massive fraud that he was unwittingly involved in.*

stare col fiato sul collo (di qualcuno)
to keep after someone
to breath down someone's neck

Stare col fiato su collo (di qualcuno) means *to keep after someone* or *to breath down someone's neck:* in other words, *to nag* or *remind someone to do something repeatedly*:

> I genitori di Carlo sono insopportabili: non si fidano di lui e **stanno** continuamente **col fiato sul suo collo.**
>
> *Carlo's parents are unbearable: they don't trust him, and they **are** constantly **keeping after him.***

avere (essere con) l'acqua alla gola
to be in a tight spot/ corner

Avere (essere con) l'acqua alla gola means *to be in a tight spot/corner*. It literally means *to have (to be with) water at your throat.* It is an expression you would use to describe a situation where there is very little room to maneuver:

> Molti comuni della Sicilia **sono con l'acqua alla gola** a causa della crisi e della conseguente mancanza di fondi.
>
> *Many Sicilian towns **are in a tight spot** because of the recession and the consequent lack of funds.*

acqua in bocca
mum's the word
keep it under your hat

Acqua in bocca literally means *water in the mouth*, but it translates as *mum's the word* or *keep it under your hat*. We use this expression when we want to tell someone to keep some information to themselves:

"Federico, hai saputo che Maria è rimasta incinta?"

"Federico, did you know that Maria got pregnant?"

"Davvero!? Ma è troppo giovane per diventare mamma!"

"Really? But she is too young to be a mother!"

"A quanto pare è una gravidanza non desiderata. Bada che nessun altro lo sappia: **acqua in bocca!**"

*"It seems to be an unwanted pregnancy. Make sure no one else finds out: **mum's the word!**"*

Idioms: games and sports
Modi di dire: giochi e sport

Sports and games play an important role in the Italian language, especially **il calcio** (*football* or *soccer*). Basketball (**il basket**) and cycling (**il ciclismo**) are also important. Many of the expressions here have found their way into the Italian language because of Italy's love for all things *calcio* and sport!

appendere le scarpe al chiodo
to hang up one's shoes

Appendere le scarpe al chiodo is an expression in sport that is used when a player retires from the game. The expression is adaptable, depending on the sport, and you can replace **le scarpe** with *skis* (**gli sci**) or any other object used in the sport. This expression can be used in other situations, too, such as retiring after years on the job.

> Dopo anni di onorata carriera, Gianni ha deciso di **appendere le scarpe al chiodo** e di abbandonare il mondo di calcio.
>
> *After a storied career, Gianni decided **to hang up his shoes** and give up football.*

essere pari e patta
to be even

Essere pari e patta means *to be even*. In other words, both sides have the same score and have drawn, as seen in our expression below:

> Stando agli ultimi sondaggi, i due soli candidati alle prossime elezioni comunali **sono pari e patta.**
>
> *According to the latest polls, the only two candidates at the next town hall election **are even.***

quando il gioco si fa duro, i duri cominciano a giocare
when the going gets tough, the tough get going

Quando il gioco si fa duro, i duri cominciano a giocare is a popular sports expression and translates as *When the going gets tough, the tough get going*. This is a common expression you will hear when the chips are down and a loss or failure is on the horizon. However, such circumstances usually push people to play/try harder!

Temevamo che la nostra squadra non vincesse la partita, ma il coach ci ricordò a gran voce che, **quando il gioco si fa duro, i duri cominciano a giocare**.

*I feared our team wouldn't win the match, but the coach loudly reminded us that **when the going gets tough, the tough get going**.*

andare/essere nel pallone
to be in a daze
to space out
to be bewildered

Andare or **essere nel pallone** means *to be in a daze, to space out, to be bewildered*, etc. It refers to someone who is confused or bewildered, usually brought on by stress, being overtired, or simply overworked:

Durante l'interrogazione, la professoressa mi fece una domanda difficile alla quale non seppi rispondere: andai totalmente nel pallone.

*During the exam, the professor asked me a difficult question that I didn't know how to respond to: I **had** completely **spaced out**.*

dare buca (a qualcuno)
to stand (someone) up

Dare buca (a qualcuno) means *to stand (someone) up*. You stand someone up when you make plans with them, but then you fail to show up without calling or letting them now.

> È la terza volta che Fabio mi **dà buca**: non gli chiederò più di uscire con me!
>
> *It is the third time Fabio **has stood me up**: I will not ask him to go out with me anymore!*

fare centro
to be right on target; to score

Fare centro is an expression you hear in a lot of sports when a player hits a target perfectly. It means *to be right on target* or *to score*. You can also use this expression in other contexts, too:

> Col nuovo piano di svilipppo l'azienda **ha fatto centro** ed ha triplicato il volume dei propri affari.
>
> *With the new development plan, the company **was right on target** and tripled the volume of their business.*

dribblare
to dribble; to avoid

Dribblare literally means *to dribble*, like in basketball. It is also used figuratively to mean *to avoid*:

> È tipico di Anna **dribblare** un problema e rimandarne la soluzione a chissà quando.
>
> *It is typical of Anna **to avoid** a problem and to put off the solution to who knows when.*

il gioco non vale la candela

the game is not worth the candle

Il gioco non vale la candela means *the game is not worth the candle*. You use this expression when you want to highlight the fact that any benefit to doing something is outweighed by the immense hassle involved!

> Mi piacerebbe molto andare in quell'agriturismo, ma i prezzi e la distanza dalla mia città sono davvero eccessivi, per cui **il gioco non vale la candela**.
>
> *I would really like to go to that vacation farm, but the prices and the distance from my city are really excessive that **the game is not worth the candle**.*

Printed in Great Britain
by Amazon.co.uk, Ltd.,
Marston Gate.